THE
WILEY
CANNING COMPANY
COOKBOOK

THE
WILEY
CANNING COMPANY
COOKBOOK

Recipes to Preserve the Seasons

CHELSEA J. O'LEARY

Foreword by
CAROLINE RANDALL WILLIAMS

BLUE
HILLS
PRESS

Publisher & Editor: Matthew Teague
Design & Layout: Lindsay Hess
Assistant Publisher: Josh Nava
Photography: Chelsea J. O'Leary
Additional Photography: Zachary Gray (pages 21 & 247) and Lauren Watt (pages 48, 49, 51, 52 & 53)
Hair & Makeup: Erica Beukelman
Copy Editor: Alexandra Callahan
Index: Jay Kreider

Blue Hills Press
P.O. Box 239
Whites Creek, TN 37189

Hardback: 978-1-951217-43-3
eBook ISBN: 978-1-951217-51-8
Library of Congress Control Number: 2022947527
Printed in China
10 9 8 7 6 5 4 3 2 1

Note: The following list contains names used in *The Wiley Canning Company Cookbook* that may be registered with the United States Copyright Office: Ball, Boeing, Dial, Johnny Apple Peeler, Luigi's Real Italian Ice, Lunchable, Mason jar, Microplane, Nissan, Oxo, Post-it, Ziploc.

The information in this book is given in good faith; however, no warranty is given, nor are results guaranteed. Portions of the canning and preserving process can be dangerous. Your safety is your responsibility. Neither Blue Hills Press nor the author assume any responsibility for injuries or accidents.

To learn more about Blue Hills Press books, or to find a retailer near you, email info@bluehillspress.com or visit us at www.bluehillspress.com.

In honor of all who came before me.

Dear Sullivan,

The heart of this book beats in rhythm with yours. Wiley Canning Company was founded when I was four months pregnant with you, and I began writing this book when I was five months pregnant with you. Then, you were a part of the physical body that created Wiley Canning Company and the pages you are reading today. Now, you are the doorway that leads me to the truest version of myself. This is the only version I wish to be as I write anything: a letter, an essay, a poem, or a cookbook. Already, the power and energy you've given me and the world around us is immeasurable.

Sullivan, I thank you every day. Without you, the woman who wrote this book would not exist. Every ounce of energy poured into this book is the energy of a mother you created. I am infinitely grateful for your crucial role in not only bringing this book to life but in bringing me new life as well.

The beauty of this book is it supports my vision to raise you to notice, honor, and celebrate an ordinary life, one that derives meaning from common, everyday occurrences. The poem below, "Do not ask your children to strive" by William Martin, captures this vision quite perfectly:

Do not ask your children
to strive for extraordinary lives.
Such striving may seem admirable,
but it is the way of foolishness.
Help them instead to find the wonder
and the marvel of an ordinary life.
Show them the joy of tasting
tomatoes, apples, and pears.
Show them how to cry
when pets and people die.
Show them the infinite pleasure
in the touch of a hand.
And make the ordinary come alive for them.
The extraordinary will take care of itself.

To be successful as your mother is to show you the dance of leaves and light as the sunshine travels through trees. It is to touch the warmth of your back during a hike in the Tennessee woods. It is to teach you about the deeply-rooted fear that permeates our beings when we listen to and chase our deepest, most precious desires—like the desire to write a book or become a mother—and to promise you we can, *and must*, move forward despite that fear. To be successful as your mother is to show you great love, and one way I wish to do this is through nourishing, delicious food—some of which you will find in the pages that follow.

The existence of this book alone can serve as your reminder that a jar of Canned Peaches can bring a moment of thrill into your kitchen. A spread of rich jams and cheeses can uplift a room full of your closest friends. A bowl of your great-grandmother's chili, made from Canned Tomatoes, can warm your body and heal an aching heart.

This, you see, is the marvel of an ordinary life.

Sullivan, I love you beyond the highest skies. I am yours, and you are mine, my tenderhearted, determined, extraordinary boy. This book is ours.

To the end of my days, I thank you.

With great love,

CONTENTS

Foreword 13

RECIPE DIRECTORY

FOREWORD

BY CAROLINE RANDALL WILLIAMS

I've written before about the truth that food tells stories. In the spirit of my dear friend's beautiful book, that truth takes on new layers of meaning. A recipe is an artifact, a record of someone else's learning and labor. It is also a best wish, a gift from its creator to the home cook who dares or the seasoned chef who stays curious. That is always true.

But what does it mean to take something fresh and decide not to prepare it for immediate consumption, but to say, *I know I will miss your flavor in times to come. I am going to find a way to keep you. To save your present loveliness in another form, that I might celebrate your abundance alongside my future joys, my future quiet moments, my future late night pantry rummagings and spoon tastings?* Well, I say that is a different kind of promise. And we've already got a word for it: *preserve.*

This book offers up a kind of magic, a kind of transcendence. When we can things, when we jar pickles, or when we labor, brow-sweated but cheerful, over a simmering pot of fruit preserves, we become time travelers. We are taking a leap of (science-backed!) faith that we have the power to create something that allows us to taste these same blackberries in the pot before us far into the future.

Canned food is survival food. Pickled flavors are will-to-live flavors. Preserved fruits are sweet time capsules—so many warmer, brighter days, right there in the tin, in the jar, to add to your here and now, to sustain and inspire you.

The Wiley Canning Company Cookbook is more than a labor of love; it is a sweet, elemental kind of history lesson, teaching us to become the happy custodians of our own kitchen memories, to turn what we've got in the present into something preserved and precious for the future. Like the ingredients it celebrates on its pages, this book is fundamental and fun, sustainable and sustaining, timely and timeless—a real gift.

INTRODUCTION

FOUNDATIONAL KNOWLEDGE

Part I

BUILD YOUR FOUNDATION

INTRODUCTION

Wiley Canning Company

Delicious ingredients lead to delicious meals. Just like us, a thoughtfully-created meal is greater than the sum of its parts.

When we have a single ingredient that is homemade and precise—like freshly-canned, locally-grown tomatoes or an in-season Peach Jam—we can create an entire meal that awakens our hearts and minds, one that sends a tingle through our jaw as we take our first bite.

Simply, the goal of this book is to, again and again, provide a *single* ingredient that elevates your meal for yourself, your family, and all who are fortunate to gather around your table. It is to provide a *single* ingredient that carefully inoculates your meal with rich history and a meaningful story.

I have created canning, pickling, and preserving recipes and shared them with you through pages of mindful words and photographs. No matter where you live—a downtown high-rise, suburban bungalow, or countryside ranch—these recipes are for you. In fact, *all* recipes were created in my downtown home in Nashville, Tennessee and enlivened any meal that included them. They will enliven your meals too. I promise you.

To fully appreciate each meal we create, we must understand that which makes it great: our commitment to the individual ingredients themselves. To fully appreciate the individual ingredients themselves—canned, pickled, and preserved fruits and vegetables—we must first rewind, walk together through history, and meet right back at this present moment. Only then can we understand the significance of the recipes in this book, including their roots, associated memories, and the ways they inadvertently reveal new meaning and value in our own lives.

Are you ready?

October in Ohio brings reminders of transition everywhere I look. High school seniors have begun their final fall semester as aluminum bleachers fill every Friday night. Stadium lights glisten as mayflies dance around their glowing hum. Red maple trees begin to live up to their name as their leaves turn vibrant crimson, and I begrudgingly accept that sticky summer days are now behind me. The Ohio skies darken each evening before I'm ready, only to soon welcome a morning chill that makes my exhale visible, reminding me my lungs are full and my breath is warm.

By this time of year, my grandfather's forearms had turned to leathery brown from a summer spent absorbing the rays of the golden sun, with one small exception. He, Grandpa Don, had a perfectly pale outline where his watch sat on his left wrist, but only we, the ones closest to him,

ever saw his bare, circular tan line. As the Ohio skies darkened each evening before he was ready, he prepared for his final harvest of the year. I knew this without having to be told because the towering corn stalks finally turned crispy and beige. This was about the time I climbed into his combine, on top of the world, and watched in awe as its huge machinery glided through thousands of waving stalks, laying his fields to rest for winter. The silos filled as my grandfather began to consider rest and celebration. We kept our fingers crossed for a healthy, fruitful harvest, and without skipping a beat, we moved onto honoring the morning of October 17 as a family, as we did every year of my life. We ate homemade chili, made from Canned Tomatoes, and chocolate chip cookies as we sat and sang at an old wooden table, and I said aloud, "*This* is my favorite meal in the world, you know."

Less than twenty miles east of where we sat, a white farmhouse stood humbly among towering

corn stalks, among acres and acres of farmland. The farmhouse was built in 1850, having no idea it would bear witness to the American Civil War, World War I, the Great Depression, and World War II. In 1920, it became the home of an agrarian family, one who would remain here for the next century, and one who, on the morning of October 17, 1935, welcomed their second child—a daughter—into the world. Gertrude Wiley, "Trudy," was born beneath the Ohio skies, as the Red maple trees began to live up to their name as their leaves turned vibrant crimson, like they would every October thereafter.

Trudy was raised as the Great Depression and World War II became inseparable frameworks of one's childhood, inseparable influences on the Wiley family's approach to living, loving, and raising children. Families remained close. Acres of flat earth turned into farmland. Farmland turned into farmed food, and farmed food turned into shelves of home canned, pickled, and preserved fruits and vegetables. Canned Tomatoes, Aristocrat Pickles, and Strawberry Jam were only a few of the canned, pickled, and preserved fruits and vegetables that became culinary mainstays in the Wiley home.

As her childhood faded and her young adult life drew near, Trudy, at twenty-three years young, met someone whose approach to living, loving, and raising children was shared. The very day they met, he had returned from a two-year draft in Germany, ready to be home beneath the Ohio skies.

Less than a year later, on Valentine's Day weekend, this man stood at the end of an aisle as he married the second child—a daughter—of an agrarian family, Trudy. She wore a traditional ivory gown, and he wore a straightforward, well-pressed suit. His sleeves were *just* long enough to cover the perfectly pale outline where his watch sat on his left wrist, only the ones closest to him ever saw. Together, they built a simple life, one focused on farming and family, less than twenty miles west of the white farmhouse that stood humbly among towering corn stalks, among acres and acres of farmland.

Today, it is my Grandma Trudy's homemade chili, made from Canned Tomatoes, and chocolate chip cookies I crave and covet. It is the morning of October 17, 1935 we honor year after year—her birthday—as we keep our fingers crossed for a healthy, fruitful harvest. It is she, Trudy Wiley, who inspired Wiley Canning Company.

Wiley Canning Company is built upon a family legacy of land stewardship, home food preservation, and meals shared around a table. *The Wiley Canning Company Cookbook* is my ode and "thank you" to all who came before me. It is my way of carrying forward all that I treasure about my family's approach to living, loving, and raising children. Every recipe that flows from *The Wiley Canning Company Cookbook* is rooted in my family's history, traditions, and values. Every recipe intends to provide that *single* ingredient that elevates your meal for yourself, your family, and all who are fortunate enough to gather around your table.

A Personal Note

The good news is, simply by reading these words at this very moment, you already know so much about me. Who and what I value, and how I wish to live, brought us here. These truths are the result of my upbringing, lessons learned, and countless thin slices of luck.

I was born and raised by my mother and father in central Ohio alongside two sisters, two sets of grandparents, miles of green land, and endless, unobstructed sky. My maternal grandparents were both raised by agrarian families and were farmers themselves. This heritage significantly impacted how I grew up. *Of course*, we would live in the Ohio countryside. *Of course*, we would eat strawberries every spring, savor sweet corn every summer, and make the majority of our meals at home. *Of course*, my first job would be on my grandparents' farm. An agricultural path had been forged by many before me with whom I share my blood, and my family did not stray from this lifestyle as each generation was born anew.

There was, however, one exception. My mother was the first of her immediate family to veer from familial farming customs when she bravely chose to become a teacher instead. She remained rooted in our family's history, traditions, and values as she carried forward all she personally treasured: an unmoving commitment to hard work, the prioritization of delicious, homemade food, and the care and regeneration of the land upon which we lived. She tweaked what she noticed needed improvement and left behind what she saw as no longer needed at all. In doing so, she left the world—*her* world—better than she found it. By living each day in a way that left her

world better than she found it, she pursued a life of generational improvement, progression, and *aliveness*.

I, too, wish to be brave. I, too, wish to leave the world—*my* world—better than I found it. To me, this also means studying my family history through a present-day lens and choosing wisely what to carry forward, what to tweak, and what to leave behind. As a granddaughter, daughter, and now mother, I, too, must pursue a life of generational improvement, progression, and *aliveness*.

"What makes *me* come alive?" I ask.

There is one thing I know for certain. Wiley Canning Company highlights what I treasure most about my family's history, traditions, and values. Through Wiley, I, too, will carry forward an unmoving commitment to hard work, the prioritization of delicious, homemade food, and the care and regeneration of the land upon which I live—just like my mother, her mother, and all the mothers and fathers who came before us with whom we share our blood. The practice of canning, pickling, and preserving is what fills my lungs. The practice of canning, pickling, and preserving is what makes *me* come alive.

The Wiley Canning Company Cookbook may serve as a reminder to wake up each day, plant two feet on the ground, and pursue that which fills *your* lungs, that which makes *you* come alive.

Let us create ingredients that lead to delicious meals alongside one another. And as we do, let us feel more alive than ever.

Canning, Pickling, and Preserving: Why They Matter Today

I believe today, more than ever, canning, pickling, and preserving are important and responsible practices.

In his book, *Art & Energy: How Culture Changes*, author Barry Lord ignited my curiosity about the relationship between canning, pickling, and preserving and our present day. In it, he discusses how human creativity is deeply tied to our natural and cultural resources at a given time. In other words, what humans create is inextricable from our accessible resources. Furthermore, what humans create directly affects the culture that subsequently emerges.

For example, soon after we discovered coal, we created massive factories, and a culture of production was born. When we discovered oil,

we created a globalized economy, and a culture of consumption was born. Today, with the discovery of renewable resources, we are creating wind energy, solar energy, and sustainable agriculture. Thus, we are cultivating a culture of *stewardship*—the stewardship of Earth, our communities, and ourselves (Lord 2014). We are gradually slowing and reevaluating once large, fast, and exploitative industries and practices. As we do this, we reconnect with and protect the resources that allow us to exist at all: natural and renewable resources.

Today, in this new millennium, canning, pickling, and preserving are three ways we can engage in stewardship of Earth, our communities, and ourselves. Today is the right time in history for a modern resurgence of canning, pickling, and preserving. Each is a skill that allows us to reduce our personal food waste. Each encourages us to create an efficient supply chain of food by sourcing our fruits and vegetables locally. Each allows us to create delicious ingredients that lead to delicious meals.

How to Use *The Wiley Canning Company Cookbook*

01   *Begin.* It sounds simple, but it can be the hardest part.

02   **Trust my guidance.** Every recipe is written in accordance with the National Center for Home Food Preservation. I am obedient to the science upon which safe canning, pickling, and preserving are built. All processing times are thoroughly researched and confidently recommended.

03   **Use this cookbook as *one* tool in your culinary toolkit.** It is my belief that I cannot and *ought not* cover every detail of any given area. Surround yourself with many minds and skillsets. Allow mine to be only one.

04   **I will not ask you to read this book cover to cover.** I *will* ask you to read The Science and Safety of Canning on page 36 and each chapter opener before diving into your first recipe. I ask this of you because I am sure that reading these pages will awaken your personal intuition when making each recipe. Reading them will give you a holistic understanding of how exactly you will transform a fresh tomato from the farmers' market into a delicious meal.

05   **Remind yourself that a *chosen* canning practice today is low-risk.** If for any reason you doubt the safety of your canned good, you can place it in the refrigerator or dispose of it right away.

06   **Personalize each recipe, if you wish.** I tell you how under the Make It Your Own section of each recipe.

07   *Get messy!* Scribble notes to yourself. Add Post-it notes. Dog ear your favorite pages. Do not try to keep this book precious.

08   **Be *so* proud.** You are improving the world within and around you—Earth, your community, *and yourself.*

09   **Finally, reach out to me with any questions as you use this book.** You can email me at hello@wileycanningcompany.com. Chances are I will see your email in my kitchen as I'm making a recipe with my son in my line of sight, a candle burning, and windows open.

Technically speaking, follow the steps below before making each recipe.

01   **Take a look around your kitchen.** Make sure it's a space in which you're ready to spend time. *Mise en place.* This is our shared motto. It means "everything in its place."

02   **Prepare your ingredients, and read the full recipe.** Set your ingredients out, and make sure you have every item you need before getting started. Read through each step of the recipe to learn your landscape ahead.

FOUNDATIONAL KNOWLEDGE

A Brief History of American Farmland

To understand our work and our pursuit of it, we must further understand ourselves. To understand ourselves, we must further understand our ancestral history. Therefore, at Wiley Canning Company, I prioritize historical research and continued education. As part of an agrarian family, this includes the study of farmland, crops, and Native peoples who once occupied the land that raised me.

One could argue the history of American farmland alone can tell the story of America. The discovery, inhabitation, and ownership of farmland cast a spotlight on the lives and lands of Native peoples and their struggle against European colonialism. Here, we could intricately examine a yearly timeline of American farmland. In 1785, for example, less than a decade after America declared its

independence from Great Britain, the Philadelphia Society for the Promotion of Agriculture was founded. Shortly thereafter, in 1793, the famed invention of the cotton gin catalyzed agricultural progression for decades to come (USDA 2000).

But, the best way to start as individuals is to take a historical dive into our *own* personal history, examining the land beneath *us*. From there, we can expand this research to the land beneath those closest to us. Little by little, we can establish a knowledge-based reverence for all who came before us, including those who made it possible to consume the fruits and vegetables grown on our surrounding land today.

The farmland that grew the food I was raised seeing, smelling, and tasting in central Ohio is land once inhabited by the Algonquian and Iroquois Nations. The name *Ohio* comes from the Iroquois word, *ohi:yo,* meaning "great river" (Ohio History Connection, n.d.).

The Algonquian Nation includes the Shawnee, Delaware, Miami, and Ottawa Tribes, and the Iroquois Nation includes the Wyandotte and Seneca-Cayuga, or Mingo, Tribes (PBS Western Reserve 2004). When these nations inhabited central Ohio, the land was extremely flat, made of contiguous plains. The same is true today.

Due to the topography of the land, the Iroquois Nation became a nation of farmers. They created and grew the *Three Sisters*, a compatible crop triad of corn, beans, and squash, still grown together today. These crops grew and thrived on Native lands. They were, therefore, key staples of Native diets.

The Shawnee Tribe was the largest tribe to inhabit Ohio's native lands beginning in the 17th century. A renowned Shawnee Chief, Tecumseh, was born in 1768 in Chalahgawtha, known today as Chillicothe, Ohio. Tecumseh is a respected and celebrated Indigenous leader due to his lifelong pursuit of tribal unity and land preservation. He pursued the health and independence of all Native peoples throughout his forty-five-year-long life, including fighting against the United States in Tecumseh's War, the Battle of Tippecanoe, and the War of 1812 as an ally to Great Britain.

Until his death in 1813 at the Battle of Thames, Tecumseh was fully dedicated to the protection, preservation, and liberty of Native lands, Native ways of living, the Shawnee Tribe, and the great Algonquian Nation (Eckert 1993; Greenspan 2018).

Today, as we source fruits and vegetables to can, pickle, and preserve, what questions can we ask?

Why might a specific crop successfully grow on our surrounding land?

What is this crop's origin story?

Who once inhabited the land that grows this crop? How might we honor this history?

To learn more about the history of American farmland, crops, and Native peoples, visit Resources on page 236.

A Brief History of American Gardening

You can grow an entire garden from the seeds of one tomato.

The sentiment above is one I often repeated as I wrote *The Wiley Canning Company Cookbook*. It communicates we need only a seed, a small spark, to ultimately create a long-lasting entity, one of great value and sustenance. When we bravely put one foot in front of the other, without any promise of what the future might hold, we soon find ourselves standing at the foot of our gardens remembering the day we began with *only* a seed and wished for what we have right now.

Clayton Brascoupé, a native Mohawk and Anishnabeg, is who first introduced this sentiment to me. I learned of Brascoupé in *The Earth Knows My Name: Food, Culture, and Sustainability in the Gardens of Ethnic Americans* by renowned author Patricia Klindienst. *The Earth Knows My Name* explores the stories and gardening practices of Native peoples like Brascoupé, European immigrants, and Asian immigrants.

Today, many choose to grow personal gardens to sustainably grow and consume fruits, vegetables, and herbs. Many choose this to eat more

economically. Many choose this to create rich environments for endangered pollinating species. Many choose this to improve water retainment or drainage on their personal properties. Many choose this ornamentally.

Most importantly though, many feel a personal garden is no choice at all; gardening is the *only* way they can carry forward their cultural heritage, relationship with the land beneath them, and sense of self and belonging. As many Native and ethnic gardeners grow fruits and vegetables, they tell the story of *who* they are through seeds that can speak a thousand words. In *The Earth Knows My Name*, Brascoupé tells Klindienst, "The garden was a way of preserving our identity. Especially if the garden contained the seeds that were given to us by our elders. It meant we kept that relationship to the earth" (Klindienst 2006). When nearly all else was lost, seeds remained. Therefore, identities remained. Klindienst writes, "What are seeds, that people carry them thousands of miles to an unknown land and treat them as if they were kin? What have we forgotten about food that people of traditional cultures remember when they regard a meal as a ritual offering?" (Klindienst 2006). We can show reverence to the voices of seeds as we grow our own gardens today.

American gardening began as—and remains—a sacred, storytelling practice in essence. It continued nationwide due to necessity for daily food. Throughout the eighteenth and first half of the nineteenth centuries, grocery stores and local markets did not yet exist. Personal and community gardens were the primary avenues to nutritious and medicinal fruits, vegetables, and herbs. As grocery stores and local markets began to popularize in the second half of the nineteenth century, gardens very slowly became less integral to daily life; they very slowly became more leisurely. Enter the genesis and rise of ornamental gardens in addition to edible gardens. Today, we grow gardens due to necessity *or* by choice. We can do so in our backyards, windowsills, greenhouses, and technologically progressive structures, such as hydroponic towers.

As we engage in modern-day gardening, let us remember it is built upon a foundation of Native and ethnic history. Today, seeds are abundant. They are no less sacred, and they contain no fewer words.

What can we learn from seeds, you and I? What history can we honor as we step into our backyards or stand drenched in the sunlight of our windowsills? What stories might come alive as we grow an entire garden from the seeds of one tomato?

A Brief History of Canning

1800s

As many methods do, the canning method began out of necessity. Near the end of the eighteenth century, France was in a period of political and social unrest. As the French Revolution led to the Napoleonic Wars, leader Napoleon Bonaparte sought to feed his large armies safely and reliably. At a time when there wasn't a tried-and-true way to do so, Napoleon offered a monetary reward to anyone who developed a method to preserve food at a large scale.

Enter *Nicolas Appert*, a Parisian chef. At the turn of the nineteenth century, Appert rose to Napoleon's challenge. He discovered the combination of heating and sealing in an airtight container assuredly decreased the risk of bacterial growth. Therefore, it decreased the risk of illness. This allowed food to be widely *and safely* saved for several months at a time (Sullivan, n.d.a).

As you might expect, this discovery was quickly shared, adopted, and industrialized. Throughout the 1800s, the tin can, industrial canning, and the Mason jar were created, supported, and widely used. In 1880, the company we know today as Ball was founded in Buffalo, New York (Ball, n.d.).

1900s

The need for safely canned food increased in the twentieth century as world wars continued. During World War I specifically, the demand for high-caloric, proteinaceous, and transportable food grew exponentially. Although glass jars were primarily used in the nineteenth century, the tin can was widely used in the twentieth century because it was cheaper to manufacture and, of course, less fragile. Home canning soared as well, and food preservation supplies were produced on a massive scale.

This was also the time period we learned, oftentimes at great cost, about factors that significantly affect the canning process and its safety, such as altitude and pressure, food acidity, and *Clostridium botulinum,* the bacterium that leads to botulism. It wasn't until 1988 that the USDA published its first guide to canning safely at home and 1993 until the FDA published its first Food Code (Sullivan, n.d.b).

2000s

The canning industry today operates at its largest scale yet—globally, nationally, and locally. Home canning, once considered a necessity, is now a chosen at-home practice for many. Large corporations, such as Ball and its subsidiaries, continue to produce home canning supplies, and home canners now share personal methods, recipes, and stories through cookbooks, online resources, and social media.

Safety measures taken in the nineteenth and twentieth centuries, such as properly heating, sealing, and pressurizing, are still taken today. Above all else, the highest priority of the canning industry, including Wiley Canning Company, is safety. The highest priority of a personal, chosen canning practice, in my eyes, is the honoring and celebration of the ordinary, joy, and *aliveness.*

Compare and Contrast: Canning, Pickling, and Preserving

As we use *The Wiley Canning Company Cookbook*, we also use a shared language. As we use a shared language, it's essential to consistently define and experience key terms and phrases. For example, when I use the word *marmalade*, I am referring to preserved citrus, including the rind, with the addition of heat and sugar. Before we fully dive into the pages that follow, let us set our vocabulary stage. Let us ensure we are using major key terms, such as canning, pickling, and preserving, consistently.

Canning is *a method* that allows us to save fruits and vegetables in a sealed, airtight container for an extended period of time. To safely save our food in a sealed, airtight container, we must follow a specific method that focuses heavily on temperature, pressure, the manipulation of each, and their direct relationship. We can manipulate the temperature and pressure using a **water-boiling canning pot**. By properly manipulating the temperature and *internal* pressure of our containers, we can create a seal that is airtight and, most importantly, safeguarded against bacterial growth. A fruit or vegetable is properly canned *only when* it is in a sealed, airtight container.

Canning recipes, such as Canned Peaches, can include whole, halved, sliced, chopped, or puréed fruits and vegetables. Additionally, canning recipes can include only the extracted juice of a fruit or vegetable, such as Canned Tomato Juice. They do

not require the addition of acid or sugar. Although, acid and sugar are often used in practice to increase the safety of a recipe.

Pickling is a category of canning that uses **heat and acid** to save a fruit or vegetable for an extended period of time. That acid, almost always, is a vinegar such as distilled white vinegar or apple cider vinegar and must be at least 5% acidic.

Pickling recipes, such as Tangy Dill Pickles, can include whole, halved, quartered, or chopped fruits and vegetables and the addition of heat and acid. If a pickling recipe uses a water-boiling canning pot to create a sealed, airtight container, it is a recipe that results in *properly canned* pickles.

Preserving is a category of canning that uses **heat and sugar** to save a fruit or vegetable for an extended period of time. There are two types of sugar at play: the fruit's **natural** sugar and our **added** sugar. The fruit's natural sugar is called *pectin*. Our added sugar is typically cane sugar. However, substitutes for cane sugar, such as monk fruit sweetener, maple syrup, or chia seeds, are often used.

Preserving recipes, such as Blackberry Lavender Jam, can include whole, halved, chopped, or puréed fruits and vegetables and the addition of heat and sugar. Additionally, preserving recipes can include only the extracted juice of a fruit or vegetable and the addition of heat and sugar. We often see preserving recipes as jams, jellies, and marmalades. Jam is made using chopped or puréed fruits and vegetables and the addition of heat and sugar. Jelly is made using a fruit or vegetable's juice and the addition of heat and sugar. Marmalade is made from using whole citrus, including the rind, and the addition of heat and sugar. You will find jam and marmalade recipes in *The Wiley Canning Company Cookbook*. If a preserving recipe uses a water-boiling canning pot to create a sealed, airtight container, it is a recipe that results in *properly canned* preserves.

The root word *preserven,* meaning "to keep safe or free from harm", is also used in the all-encompassing term, **preservation,** that describes many ways of safely saving our food at home, including canning, pickling, preserving, freezing, and more.

The Science and Safety of Canning

We bear witness to the scientific principles that underlie canning in our everyday lives. If you've opened a can of soda on a summer day, felt a tingle through your jaw as you've sipped cold water with fresh lemon juice, or enjoyed the sweetness of a lollipop, then you've experienced the scientific principles of canning, pickling, and preserving. The audible *"pssh!"* we hear when we open a can of soda is indicative of the high internal pressure of a sealed, airtight container. The tingle that travels through our jaw as we sip cold water with lemon juice is a sign of its low pH level, or *acidity*. The molecular bonds created between water and sugar molecules is what creates long-lasting candy.

Understanding the science of canning increases our own intuition when bringing a recipe to life. In other words, understanding the science of canning allows us to be more independent, confident home food preservers. When we feel more independent and confident, we're able to feel ease and *joy* more readily. For example, once we've memorized the route to our favorite restaurant or park, we're able to enjoy our commute there. We turn up our music. We call our best friend and ask, "Whatcha doin'?" We process a conversation we had with our partner the previous evening. Indeed, understanding leads to ease or joy; these are essential feelings to capture when saving our food at home each season.

In this section, I've broken down the science of canning into three major categories: biology, chemistry, and physics. When canning, these sciences matter greatly *in combination*. The physics of canning builds upon the biology and chemistry of canning. The safety of a canned good is then directly related to the science that occurs *within* that canned good. By understanding these sciences, you will learn exactly how we come alive as biologists, chemists, and physicists when we can, pickle, and preserve fruits and vegetables.

THE BIOLOGY

Most simply stated, biology is the study of life or living organisms. The main reason we care so much about the biology of canning is **it is our ultimate goal to eliminate living organisms inside our sealed, airtight containers in order for their contents to be safe to consume.*** It is imperative we understand exactly how life is sustained and eliminated—specifically the lives of microorganisms such as bacteria—when canning, pickling, and preserving food.

To live and thrive on Earth, most living organisms require access to water (H_2O) and oxygen (O_2). As long as microorganisms have access to water and oxygen, their *only* goal is to survive and reproduce. So, we must make it impossible for them to do so. We must eliminate their access to water and oxygen inside of our sealed, airtight containers.

How do we eliminate their access to water and oxygen inside of our sealed, airtight containers? Let's begin with water. We very purposefully bind water molecules to *other* molecules, such

*The fermentation process uses microorganisms, such as yeast, to convert carbohydrates into alcohols or acids, such as lactic acid, in an anaerobic environment.

*This describes the energy of most, but not all, gases on Earth.

as sugar, in order for them to be *inaccessible* to microorganisms. When we add sugar to a pot of crushed blackberries, for example, that sugar searches for, finds, and holds onto the water molecules of those crushed berries. There are no longer miniature pools of water molecules; each water molecule (H_2O) has been claimed.

Now let's turn our attention to oxygen. Again, we very purposefully eliminate any subtle pockets of air, or oxygen, within our sealed, airtight containers. When you are directed to remove air bubbles before you process your Blackberry Lavender Jam, for example, your inner biologist reads, "Revoke microorganisms' access to oxygen." When we drive excess air out of our jars via processing in our water-boiling canning pot, our inner biologist knows we are driving out microorganisms' access to oxygen.

When we eliminate microorganisms' access to water and oxygen, we eliminate their ability to survive and reproduce. Though, we might ask, "But what about recipes that do *not* include the addition of sugar?" There are alternative and additional ways we can eliminate microorganisms' ability to survive and reproduce, which leads us to...*the chemistry* of canning.

THE CHEMISTRY

Microorganisms are both intelligent and creative. In highly-deprived environments, they can often find a way to evolve *just enough* to survive and reproduce. However, even the most intelligent and creative living organisms require a certain set of conditions to live and thrive. One condition, as you read above, includes access to water and oxygen. A second condition is a relatively neutral

Foundational Knowledge | PART I: BUILD YOUR FOUNDATION

environment. When we create the opposite of a neutral environment—an *extreme* environment—we again make it impossible for microorganisms to live and thrive. When canning, pickling, and preserving, we very purposefully create extreme environments within our containers such as highly acidic, extremely hot or cold, and highly pressurized environments.

To create highly acidic environments, we add an acid. Vinegar, lemon juice, ascorbic acid, and citric acid decrease microorganisms' ability to live and thrive by creating an environment that is highly acidic. The way we measure the acidity of an environment is by measuring its pH. The pH of any fruit,

vegetable, or canned good will fall between 0.0 and 14.0. A neutral fruit, vegetable, or environment will measure at 7.0. Any measurement below 7.0 is considered acidic. Any measurement above 7.0 is considered alkaline, or *basic.* Vinegars, lemon juice, ascorbic acid, and citric acid have a pH between 2.0 and 3.0. Thus, when one is added to any recipe, the recipe lowers in pH, or increases in acidity, and becomes more protected against microorganisms.

If vinegar, lemon juice, ascorbic acid, and citric acid create an acidic environment, how can we create an environment that is extreme in pressure and temperature? This is the point at which we dive into...*the physics!*

THE PHYSICS

When an environment is extremely high- or low-pressure, it is impossible for microorganisms to survive and reproduce. Secondly, when an environment is extremely hot or cold, it is impossible for microorganisms to survive and reproduce.

When canning, pickling, and preserving, there is *one* equation that explains how we create an environment that is extreme in both pressure and temperature. This equation also explains how pressure and temperature work together to create a sealed, airtight, *and safe* container. It's called the Ideal Gas Law. I refer to it as *The Canning Equation*. It is below.

$$PV = nRT$$

P stands for **pressure**.

V stands for **volume**.

n stands for **number**, or amount, of substance.

R is the **Ideal Gas Constant**, $8.3145 \, J \cdot K^{-1} \cdot mol^{-1}$. This is *not* a value you must memorize. You must only know it is unchanging; it is always $8.3145 \, J \cdot K^{-1} \cdot mol^{-1}$.*

T stands for **temperature**.

P, again, stands for **pressure**. This is a variable we can *and do* manipulate while canning. Let's circle **P**.

$$(\text{P}) \, V = nRT$$

V, as we know, stands for **volume**. When we can, pickle, and preserve fruits and vegetables, we work with solid containers made of glass and steel. Our jars, lids, and rings do not expand like balloons throughout the canning process. The volume of our containers does not change; it is **fixed**. Let's hide **V**.

$$(\text{P}) \, \cancel{V} = nRT$$

n, the **number**, or amount, of substance is also fixed throughout this process. Once we fill our jars with jam, for example, the amount of jam inside of our jars remains the same. We are not pumping jam in or out of our jars as we process them. Let's hide **n**.

$$(\text{P}) \, \cancel{V} = \cancel{n}RT$$

Remember **R**, the **Ideal Gas Constant**, is always $8.3145 \, J \cdot K^{-1} \cdot mol^{-1}$. It is a fixed value. Let's hide **R**.

$$(\text{P}) \, \cancel{V} = \cancel{nR}T$$

Finally, we already know **T** stands for **temperature**, and we, of course, can *and do* manipulate temperature while canning. Let's circle **T**.

$$(\text{P}) \, \cancel{V} = \cancel{nR} \, (\text{T})$$

Pressure = Temperature

Pressure *equals* temperature. In other words, whatever happens to **P** *must* also happen to **T**. Whatever happens to **T** *must* also happen to **P**. They are *equal*. When we increase the temperature of our canned good, we also increase its internal pressure. When we decrease the temperature of our canned good, we also decrease its internal pressure.

We use our water-boiling canning pot to manipulate temperature and pressure. When we process our jars, we take two crucial steps:

01 **We create an environment that is extremely hot.** We *boil* our jars. When we create an environment that is extremely hot, we simultaneously create an environment with a high internal pressure. These extremes, alone *and* in tandem, make it impossible for microorganisms to survive and reproduce.

02 **We manipulate pressure and temperature to create a sealed, airtight container.** First, we increase the temperature and internal pressure of our jars by processing them in our water-boiling canning pot. Then, we remove our jars from our water-boiling canning pot and allow them to cool *or decrease in temperature*. When the temperature of our jars decreases, the internal pressure of our jars also decreases. As the internal pressure decreases inside of our jars, it creates an internal vacuum, pulling the lid down quickly and tightly, and seals our jars.

WATER-BOILING PROCESSING

Jars ready to be processed

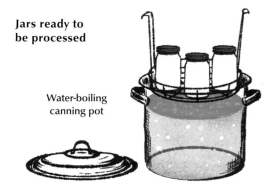

Water-boiling canning pot

Jars processing in boiling water

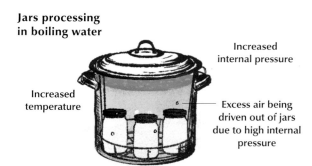

Increased temperature

Increased internal pressure

Excess air being driven out of jars due to high internal pressure

Jars cooling

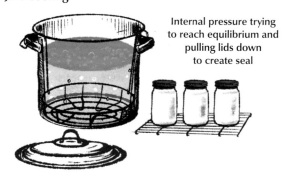

Internal pressure trying to reach equilibrium and pulling lids down to create seal

THE SAFETY

The safety of our canned goods is inextricably linked to *the science*. When we do our best to remove all microorganismal growth and create a sealed, airtight container, we do our best to create *a safe* canned good.

When it's time to enjoy our canned, pickled, and preserved fruits and vegetables, there is a set of final questions to ask ourselves as we open our jars:

01　**Is our jar physically damaged in any way?** If so, compost it right away.

02　**Are gaseous bubbles present?** If so, compost it right away.

03　**Is there significant pressure build-up inside of our jars?** In other words, is the lid bulging, or it it leaking? If so, open it outside and facing away from you, and compost it right away.

04　**Is there visible microorganismal growth such as mold?** If so, compost it right away.

Remember, if for any reason you doubt the safety of your canned good, you can discard or compost it right away.

You've got this!

ALTITUDE

If you process your canned, pickled, and preserved fruits and vegetables at an altitude higher than 1,000 feet, you must increase your processing time.

Once your jars are ready to be processed and submerged in your water-boiling canning pot, adjust your processing time as follows:

Altitude Feet	Increase Processing Time
1,001- 3,000	5 minutes
3,001- 6,000	10 minutes
6,001- 8,000	15 minutes
8,001-10,000	20 minutes

Produce Calendar

The produce calendar that follows is representative of Tennessee. I often find my family in Ohio is about one month behind us. I recommend you make a note—right here in this book!—of the fruits and vegetables you see at your local farmers' market and apply it to your personal canning seasons. As you read in How to Use *The Wiley Canning Company Cookbook*, I encourage you to *get messy*. Scribble notes to yourself. Add Post-it notes. This book is not intended to remain precious.

JANUARY	FEBRUARY	MARCH	APRIL	MAY	JUNE
• Herbs	• Herbs	• Herbs	• Herbs	• Carrots	• Apples
		• Radishes	• Radishes	• Herbs	• Beets
				• Onions	• Blackberries
				• Radishes	• Blueberries
				• Raspberries	• Carrots
				• Strawberries	• Cherries
					• Corn
					• Cucumbers
					• Garlic
					• Green beans
					• Herbs
					• Onions
					• Radishes
					• Raspberries
					• Peaches
					• Plums
					• Strawberries
					• Tomatoes

JULY	AUGUST	SEPTEMBER	OCTOBER	NOVEMBER	DECEMBER
• Apples	• Apples	• Apples	• Apples	• Apples	• Carrots
• Apricots	• Apricots	• Beets	• Beets	• Beets	• Herbs
• Beets	• Beets	• Blackberries	• Carrots	• Carrots	
• Blackberries	• Blueberries	• Corn	• Green beans	• Herbs	
• Blueberries	• Corn	• Cucumbers	• Herbs	• Radicchio	
• Cherries	• Cucumbers	• Herbs	• Muscadines	• Radishes	
• Corn	• Garlic	• Green beans	• Pears	• Tomatoes	
• Cucumbers	• Green beans	• Muscadines	• Peppers		
• Garlic	• Herbs	• Pears	• Radicchio		
• Green beans	• Muscadines	• Peppers	• Radishes		
• Herbs	• Onions	• Plums	• Tomatoes		
• Onions	• Peaches (Early August)	• Radicchio			
• Peaches	• Pears	• Radishes			
• Peppers	• Plums	• Tomatoes			
• Plums	• Peppers				
• Radishes	• Raspberries				
• Raspberries	• Tomatoes				
• Tomatoes					

Equipment and Tools

CANNING EQUIPMENT

Processing
- Water-boiling canning pot
- Rack or trivet

Jars
- 8-ounce canning jars
- 16-ounce regular-mouth canning jars
- 16-ounce wide-mouth canning jars
- 32-ounce regular-mouth canning jars
- 32-ounce wide-mouth canning jars
- Regular-mouth jar lids
- Wide-mouth jar lids
- Regular-mouth jar rings
- Wide-mouth jar rings

Aids
- Jar lifter
- Wide-mouth funnel

STORAGE
- Storage container for rings
- Storage container for unused lids
- Storage container for used lids
- Freezer bags

ADDITIONAL
- Notebook
- Pen or pencil
- Labels
- Permanent marker

KITCHEN TOOLS AND UTENSILS
- Kitchen scale
- Pots and pans
- Candy or meat thermometer
- Large bowls
- Large strainer or colander
- Fine mesh strainer or sieve
- Baking sheets
- Measuring cups
- Measuring spoons
- Vegetable brush
- Cutting board
- Knives
- Vegetable peeler
- Apple peeler and corer
- Cherry pitter
- Melon baller
- Microplane
- Blender
- Silicone spatula
- Wooden spoon
- Potato masher
- Ladle
- Tongs
- Splatter screen
- Hand towels
- Drying mat
- Oven mitts
- Potholders

Pantry Staples

VINEGARS

- Apple cider vinegar, 5% acidity
- Distilled white vinegar, 5% acidity
- Red wine vinegar, 5% acidity
- Rice vinegar, 5% acidity
- White wine vinegar, 5% acidity

SALTS, SUGARS, AND SPICES

- Alum
- Black peppercorns
- Canning or pickling salt
- Cinnamon sticks
- Chia seeds
- Dill seed
- Fennel seed
- Ground allspice
- Ground mustard seed
- Monk fruit sweetener
- Mustard seed
- Nutmeg
- Pectin
- Red pepper flakes
- Whole allspice
- Whole cloves
- Sugar

EXTRACTS AND PASTES

- Coconut extract
- Lavender extract
- Peppermint extract
- Vanilla bean paste

ACIDIFIERS

- Lemon and lime juice
- Acetic acid
- Citric acid

Routines, Tips, and Tricks

SETTING UP YOUR WATER-BOILING CANNING POT

01 **Allow yourself 30–45 minutes to set up your water-boiling canning pot and prepare your kitchen.** Now is the time to light a new candle, open a window, and turn up a favorite playlist.

02 **Confidently begin with a clean canning pot, rack, jars, rings, and lids.**

03 **Fill your canning pot with water, and place it on your stove.**

04 **Place your rack inside your canning pot.** *Do not yet submerge your rack.*

05 **Place the jars and rings on top of the rack.** Submerge the rack, jars, and rings, allowing the jars to completely fill with water. Ensure the water level is ultimately at least 1 inch above your jars.

06 **Place your lid on your canning pot, and bring to a boil.** Boil your jars and rings for 5 minutes. This step sterilizes your jars.*

07 **Place your lids in a saucepan or small pot.** Boiling water may harm the engineered sealant on your lids, so sterilize your lids by placing them in 180°F, or 83°C, water for 5 minutes. You can use your candy or meat thermometer to gauge the water's temperature.

08 **As your jars, rings, and lids are sterilizing, place a drying mat or hand towel, laid flat, next to your stove at a safe distance.** This is where you will allow your jars, rings, and lids to cool.

*When a recipe requires a processing time of 10 or more minutes, the proactive sterilization of jars, rings, and lids is not required (National Center for Home Food Preservation 2017). However, it is my personal practice to sterilize jars, rings, and lids for any recipe that will be stored outside of a refrigerator or freezer for an extended period. If only inner peace is the measurable outcome of this choice, it is worth it.

REGULAR-MOUTH JARS VS. WIDE-MOUTH JARS

It is important to pay close attention to the *type* of jar required for a recipe. The size of the jar's mouth—regular or wide—matters greatly in certain instances. For example, regular-mouth jars aid in keeping fruits and vegetables submerged in their water, syrup, or brine. If a fruit or vegetable floats above its water, syrup, or brine, it gains access to the small gap of air, or oxygen, that

exists between the top of your liquid and the lid of your jar. As you read in The Science and Safety of Canning, that fruit or vegetable becomes susceptible to microorganismal growth and oxidation when it floats above its water, syrup, or brine. We depend heavily on the size of our jar's mouth to keep our fruits and vegetables submerged and *safe*.

HOW TO CORE FRUITS AND VEGETABLES

You can core your fruits and vegetables using a variety of approaches and tools. Follow your personal curiosity, and allow yourself to identify your *own* preferences for coring your favorite fruits and vegetables. My preliminary guidance is below.

01   **Use a paring knife.** Paring knives work best for coring tomatoes and strawberries. Rotate your paring knife in a circular motion around the stem of the fruit or vegetable to fully loosen and separate the core. Remove the core using your fingers or the assistance of your knife.

02   **Use a melon baller.** Melon ballers work best for coring pears. Rotate your melon baller in a circular motion around and beneath the core of your pear. Your melon baller will allow you to smoothly remove the core.

03   **Use your hands.** Our hands work best for apricots, peaches, and plums. They also work best to remove small seeds, such as the seeds of muscadines and citrus fruits. Once you've cut your apricots, peaches, plums, and muscadines into halves, remove the pit and seeds using your fingers.

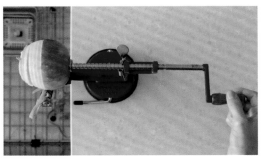

04   **Use a cherry pitter.** You can remove the pits of multiple cherries at a time using a cherry pitter. I use the OXO Good Grips Quick Release Multi-Cherry Pitter.

05   **Use an apple peeler and corer.** This is one of my favorite kitchen tools. I use the Johnny Apple Peeler.

BATHING YOUR BERRIES

When Wiley Canning Company first launched in July 2020, my mom and I created Blueberry Mint Jam together, our first-ever jam recipe. As we created and tested this recipe, she showed me a brilliant trick for bathing berries. Here's how it goes!

Put your berries in a large bowl. Fill your bowl to the very top with cool water. Your bowl should be large enough to leave 1–2 inches of water sitting above your berries. Begin to gently sift through your berries with your fingers. You'll notice loose stems, leaves, and debris begin to float to the top. Remove the excess debris (or as I call them, *floaties!*), and transfer your berries into a strainer. Rinse your berries.

Ta-dah!

HOW TO CHOOSE THE RIGHT CUCUMBERS TO PICKLE

When our goal is to create delicious, crunchy pickles, we must begin with fresh, high-quality cucumbers. It is widely advised to source Kirby cucumbers for pickling recipes. Kirby cucumbers are distinguished by their firmness and petite size. They are about 1½ inches in diameter and about 4–5 inches long, and they contain seeds. The reason Kirby cucumbers are preferrable is they provide the ever-coveted *crunch* of a delicious pickle. English, Persian, and garden cucumbers are an absolute delight, but they tend to maintain less *crunch* when used for pickles due to thinner skins. Farmers' markets are full of Kirby cucumbers every summer. I encourage you to source yours from your local farmers' market when possible.

HOW TO DETECT THE SETTING POINT OF JAM AND MARMALADE

The **setting point** of jam or marmalade is the point at which it has reached desired consistency, or viscosity. Once it has set, it is ready to be ladled into your jars and processed. A jam or marmalade's set can be tested two main ways: the drip test or freezer test.

You can conduct a drip test by dipping a spoon or spatula into your cooked jam or marmalade and holding it above your pot to observe how quickly or slowly the jam or marmalade drips. It should drip slowly but with fluidity, and each drip should become slower and slower. If it quickly and readily runs off your spoon or spatula, it has not yet set.

You can also conduct a freezer test. When you begin a jam or marmalade recipe, place a plate in the freezer. When it is time to gauge the setting point, remove the plate from the freezer, and place a spoonful of cooked jam or marmalade on your chilled plate for 2 minutes. When the jam or marmalade is nudged, it should wrinkle if it has set.

In addition to the drip test or the freezer test, you can measure the temperature of your jam or marmalade. It must reach 220°F, or 105°C, to properly set.

Rest assured, the more you make jam and marmalade, the more confident you become as a judge of their setting points.

HOW TO REDUCE AND RID OF PRODUCE WASTE

The reduction of food waste is a high priority in my personal life. Growing up, my family valued "clean plates," and this taught me an important lesson: to serve myself an amount I felt confident I could finish. Ultimately, it was not a clean plate that felt worthwhile; it was that I did not waste the food my parents prepared.

When I moved to Nashville as a twenty-three-year-old, I gained access to a plethora of phenomenal restaurants. Oftentimes, my eyes are bigger than my stomach, and I leave these restaurants with a to-go box. Now, in my adult life, I am consciously trying to not only serve myself an amount I feel confident I can finish, but I am also trying to *order* an amount I feel confident I can finish. As I've brought an increased awareness to this priority, I've learned a few tricks that seamlessly apply to canning, pickling, and preserving.

01 **Buy fresh produce in accordance with your calendar.** We want to begin each recipe with freshly-picked fruits and vegetables. In other words, we want to use our fruits and vegetables very close to the moment we source them *or* when we detect ideal ripeness. If you have *one* afternoon to dedicate to canning, pickling, or preserving, buy only the produce you feel confident you can finish that afternoon. If you have a full weekend to dedicate to canning, pickling, or preserving, buy only the produce you feel confident you can finish that weekend.

02 **Buy fresh fruits and vegetables in accordance with the supplies you have readily available.** In the height of the COVID-19 pandemic, Ball jars, lids, and rings became increasingly difficult to source. It taught me to never take access to supplies for granted. It also taught me to source my supplies *before* sourcing my fruits and vegetables. When I prepare to make a recipe, I first source my supplies. I then source my produce. This ensures I will have enough jars, rings, and lids to store my finished product.

03 **Include time and space to freeze excess fruits and vegetables as a personal practice.** I often have an extra pint or pound of any given fruit or vegetable. My first choice is to eat it fresh! If I'm unable to do so, I freeze it if possible. Freezing excess fruits and vegetables is a safe and fast way to save them longer term.

04 **Create a fancy beverage.** One of my favorite ways to use excess produce is to create an indulgent drink to sip. I almost always have remaining cucumbers when I make pickles. I slice 'em up for cucumber water or seltzer. My absolute *favorite* addition to a glass of cool water is the combination of cucumber slices and strawberries. You can also add orange, grapefruit, or peach slices to a glass of cool water. Lastly, you can add excess lemon slices to a mug of warm water in the morning to jumpstart your day *and* digestion.

05 **Create a unique vinegar.** You can use excess apple skins, for example, to make homemade apple cider vinegar.

06 **Finally, compost your excess produce.** Here in Nashville, I personally use Compost Nashville.

Part II

BECOME A
STEWARD

CANNING RECIPES

Canning—a method that allows us to save fruits and vegetables—is a rewarding, joyous, and responsible practice we can each adopt today. Each week, we might consistently tidy our home, exercise, or share a meal with close friends. These are habits, *or practices*, we incorporate into our lives to experience routine, pride, and meaning. Canning allows us to experience these things through food. I often think to myself, "I interact with food at least three times every day: breakfast, lunch, and dinner. What if each interaction provides a small sense of routine, pride, or meaning? How might that change my day? How might that change *my life?*"

In this way, canning is far bigger and greater than a method that allows us to save fruits and vegetables for an extended period of time. It is a weekly opportunity for routine, or familiarity, an experience that brings us comfort and reliability. It is a weekly sense of pride as we acknowledge we are fed, full, and loved through well-grown food. It is our weekly dose of meaning as we notice how a warm, rich meal can cut through tension, spark conversation, and foster our ever-coveted, innate need for connection. This potential is not to be underestimated. We—you and I—can generate great power through small things, things as small as a canned good.

NOTES FOR CANNING

Foundation

Before diving into your first canning recipe, I encourage you to read the following sections of this book: Compare and Contrast: Canning, Pickling, and Preserving on page 34, The Science and Safety of Canning on page 36, and Routines, Tips, and Tricks on page 48, particularly How to Core Fruits and Vegetables.

Preparation

Canning, as you know, is *a method* that allows us to save fruits and vegetables in a sealed, airtight container for an extended period of time using a water-boiling canning pot. It is important to make sure your kitchen is a space in which you're ready to spend some time before making a canning recipe. Refer to How to Use *The Wiley Canning Company Cookbook* on page 24. Each recipe ahead begins with setting up your water-boiling canning pot and sterilizing your jars, rings, and lids. Refer to Setting Up Your Water-Boiling Canning Pot on page 48.

Yield

Yield may vary. The following recipes ensure you will accomplish *at least* the yield provided.

Three main factors affect final yield when canning:

01 **The shape of our individual fruits and vegetables.** The shape may affect the way our fruits and vegetables spatially settle in our jars.

02 **The water content of our fruits and vegetables.** Ripe, well-hydrated fruits and vegetables may produce a slightly higher yield due to higher water content per fruit or vegetable.

03 **Our personal handling of our fruits and vegetables.** Canning recipes can include whole, halved, sliced, chopped, or puréed fruits and vegetables. If we cut our fruits and vegetables in half, we may fit slightly less than if we cut them into quarters.

Acidification

Many recipes ahead include ascorbic acid or lemon juice as acidifiers. Ascorbic acid is used as a short-term preservative to prevent our fruits and vegetables from bruising or browning throughout the canning process. Lemon juice is often added as an acidifier to increase the safety of a recipe. Refer to The Science and Safety of Canning on page 36. There may be an ever-so-slight citrus note to your Canned Tomatoes, Canned Tomato Juice, and Canned Tomato Sauce due to this. You may, however, substitute your lemon juice with citric acid. I recommend 2 tablespoons of lemon juice per 1 32-ounce jar, and you may substitute this with ½ teaspoon of citric acid (McClellan 2018).

Storage

Once your jars have properly sealed, I encourage you to remove your rings from your jars. Although this is not absolutely critical, there are three main reasons I encourage you to do so:

01 **You can reuse your rings for future recipes.**

02 **The removal of your rings will not affect the seals of your jars.** The lid is what creates a proper seal. The rings are simply needed to hold lids in place as they seal.

03 **Removing rings increases visibility.** You can easily see spoilage or bacterial growth inside your jars once rings have been removed.

Date your jars. Labeling can be as simple as writing the date on masking tape with a permanent marker or personalized with a label you design yourself.

Joy

Finally, I encourage you to can as many fruits and vegetables as you find achievable *and joyful*. I include a starting point in terms of produce and yield, but you will discover the effortless scalability of each recipe. As your pantry fills with food you have saved, you will fill with a sense of *aliveness*. You can trust this method, each recipe, and most importantly, yourself.

USED | REGULAR-MOUTH LIDS AND RINGS

CANNED APPLES

Steps: 15
Yield: Approximately 2 32-ounce jars

Canned Apples taste like apple pie in a jar. You can enjoy them straight out of the jar, or you can warm and serve them over vanilla ice cream with ground cinnamon on top. This recipe is simple yet incredibly rich, familiar, and comforting.

MAKE
IT YOUR
OWN

You can expect an approximate yield of 2 32-ounce jars per every 4 pounds of apples. I encourage you to can as many apples as you envision using or giving away. You can effortlessly scale this recipe by using this ratio. You can add 1 cinnamon stick or 2 to 3 whole cloves to each jar for a touch of warmth and spice at Step 08. I also use a 2:1 ratio for my syrup: 2 cups of water per 1 cup of sugar. A heavy syrup can be used as well. To create a heavy syrup, use a 2:2 ratio: 2 cups of water per 2 cups of sugar.

INGREDIENTS

4 pounds apples

20 cups water

3 teaspoons ascorbic acid

4 cups sugar

EQUIPMENT & TOOLS

2 32-ounce regular- or wide-mouth jars, rings, and lids

Water-boiling canning pot

Rack

Jar lifter

Saucepan

Thermometer

Large bowl

Measuring cups and spoons

Strainer

Apple peeler and corer

Cutting board

Knife

Large pot

Silicone spatula

Slotted spoon

Ladle

Wide-mouth funnel

Small sieve

Towel or drying rack

recipe continues

01 **Prepare your water-boiling canning pot.** Refer to Setting Up Your Water-Boiling Canning Pot on page 48.

02 **Ready your sterilized jars.** Once your canning pot has boiled for 5 minutes, remove the jars and rings. Remove lids from the saucepan. They're going to be hot to the touch, so use a jar lifter to protect your hands. Allow the jars, rings, and lids to cool.

03 **Prepare your large bowl of acidic solution.** Fill your bowl with water and ascorbic acid: 1 cup of water per ¼ teaspoon of ascorbic acid. In total, I recommend using 12 cups of water and 3 teaspoons of ascorbic acid. This solution prevents the apples from bruising or browning once they are peeled, cored, and sliced.

04 **Rinse your apples in cool water.**

05 **Peel and core your apples, then slice.** Use an apple peeler and corer. Refer to How to Core Fruits and Vegetables on page 51. Then, slice your apples. Place each peeled, cored, and sliced apple into your bowl of acidic solution. Keep your apples here until your large pot of syrup is ready.

06 **Prepare your syrup.** In your large pot, bring 8 cups of water and 4 cups of sugar to a simmer. Use your spatula to continuously stir until the sugar has dissolved completely.

07 **Briefly cook your apples.** Transfer apples to your large pot of syrup, and simmer for 5 minutes. The reason we simmer our apples in a large pot of syrup rather than water alone is to prevent bruising or browning until they are in our jars and submerged in syrup.

08 **Pack your apples.** Transfer your apples from the syrup to the jars using a slotted spoon. Tightly pack your apples.

09 **Transfer your syrup to your jars of apples.** Your syrup will be very hot, so do this carefully. Use your funnel to guide each pour, and use a ladle or a measuring cup to transfer your syrup. Fill each jar to the lowest part of the jar's mouth, about ½ inch below the rim. You may ladle your syrup over a small sieve for clearer syrup.

10 **Remove air bubbles.** If you see any bubbles in the jar, use a spatula to guide them out.

11 **Tidy up.** Wipe your jars clean, especially the rims, with a warm, damp towel.

12 **Add your lids and rings.** Tighten.

13 **Process your apples.** Submerge your jars into your water-boiling canning pot. Allow them to boil for 20 minutes. Begin your timer once the water is boiling. Adjust for altitude if needed. Refer to The Science and Safety of Canning on page 36.

14 **Cool.** Carefully remove your jars from the water using a jar lifter, and set them on a towel or drying rack to cool.

15 **Ensure they have sealed.** Once cooled, either listen for your jar to "pop," an audible indication it has sealed, or push the center of the lid to see if it pops up and down. If it *doesn't*, it's sealed! Date your jar, and store for up to a year. If the lid *does* pop up and down, it did *not* seal. Simply put that jar in your refrigerator, and enjoy within a month.

CANNED APPLESAUCE

Steps: 18
Yield: Approximately 2 32-ounce jars

Canned Applesauce was a pantry staple in our home growing up. I remember exactly where it sat in the cabinet to the left of our toaster. We ate applesauce *nearly* every day. In hindsight, it makes complete sense that it was a staple because it can be eaten any time of day—breakfast, lunch, or dinner—and it's accessible to all generations: kids, parents, and grandparents. Now, in our home, we call this "Sullivan's Spiced Applesauce" because it's his favorite Wiley recipe.

MAKE
IT YOUR
OWN

Grandma Trudy made very smooth, puréed applesauce, but I love when mine contains texture. If you are more like Grandma Trudy, I recommend using a blender to blend your cooked apples at Step 08 instead of using a potato masher.

I use sweet and semi-sweet apples, and I do not add sugar or a sweetening agent. Two of my favorite types of apples to use are Honeycrisp and Jonagold. You, however, can add sugar or a sweetening agent to taste after you've added your cinnamon at Step 10 and before you simmer at Step 11. If you add sugar or a sweetening agent, please note this may slightly increase your final yield.

I use ¾ teaspoon of cinnamon. I recommend adding ¼ teaspoon at a time and taste testing after each one. You can then decide to stop at ¼ teaspoon or ½ teaspoon. You can also add a full teaspoon of cinnamon. Lastly, you can add or substitute your favorite spice. Great substitutes or additions include ground allspice or nutmeg.

INGREDIENTS

6 pounds apples

2 tablespoons lemon juice

¾ teaspoons cinnamon

13 cups water

3 teaspoons ascorbic acid

EQUIPMENT & TOOLS

2 32-ounce regular- or wide-mouth jars, rings, and lids

Water-boiling canning pot

Rack

Jar lifter

Saucepan

Thermometer

Large bowl

Measuring cups and spoons

Strainer

Apple peeler and corer

Large pot

Silicone spatula

Ladle

Wide-mouth funnel

Towel or drying rack

recipe continues

01 **Prepare your water-boiling canning pot.** Refer to Setting Up Your Water-Boiling Canning Pot on page 48.

02 **Ready your sterilized jars.** Once your canning pot has boiled for 5 minutes, remove the jars and rings. Remove lids from the saucepan. They're going to be hot to the touch, so use a jar lifter to protect your hands. Allow the jars, rings, and lids to cool.

03 **Prepare your large bowl of acidic solution.** Fill a large bowl with water and ascorbic acid: 1 cup of water per ¼ teaspoon of ascorbic acid. In total, I recommend using 12 cups of water and 3 teaspoons of ascorbic acid. This solution prevents apples from bruising or browning once they are peeled, cored, and sliced.

04 **Rinse your apples in cool water.**

05 **Peel and core your apples, then slice.** Refer to How to Core Fruits and Vegetables on page 51. Then, slice your apples. Place each peeled, cored, and sliced apple into your bowl of acidic solution. Keep them here until you are ready to boil them.

06 **Transfer your apples to your large pot.** Cover them with 1 cup of water. Bring to a low boil. Boil for 1 minute.

07 **Cook your apples.** Reduce heat to low to medium, and simmer for 15 minutes.

08 **Mash your apples using a potato masher.**

09 **Add your lemon juice.** Once your apples are mashed, add your lemon juice tablespoon by tablespoon. Use your spatula to begin slowly stirring.

10 **Add your cinnamon.** As you continue stirring, add your cinnamon ¼ teaspoon by ¼ teaspoon.

11 **Simmer your applesauce on low for an additional 5 minutes.**

12 **Transfer your applesauce to your jars.** The applesauce will be very hot, so do this carefully. Use your funnel to guide each pour, and use a ladle or a measuring cup to transfer your applesauce. Fill each jar to the lowest part of the jar's mouth, about ½ inch below the rim.

13 **Remove air bubbles.** If you see any bubbles in the jars, use a spatula to guide them out.

14 **Tidy up.** Wipe your jars clean, especially the rims, with a warm, damp towel.

15 **Add your lids and rings.** Tighten.

16 **Process your applesauce.** Submerge your jars into the water-boiling canning pot. Allow them to boil for 20 minutes. Begin your timer once your water is boiling. Adjust for altitude if needed. Refer to The Science and Safety of Canning on page 36.

17 **Cool.** Carefully remove your jars from the water using a jar lifter, and set them on a towel or drying rack to cool.

18 **Ensure they have sealed.** Once cooled, either listen for your jar to "pop," an audible indication it has sealed, or push the center of the lid to see if it pops up and down. If it *doesn't*, it's sealed! Date your jar, and store for up to a year. If the lid *does* pop up and down, it did *not* seal. Simply put that jar in your refrigerator, and enjoy within a month.

CANNED CHERRIES

Steps: 13
Yield: Approximately 2 32-ounce jars

Canned Cherries alone enrich my entire pantry. I appreciate how each cherry retains its original shape, and I admire how each jar is the color of merlot. You can enjoy Canned Cherries atop pastries and yogurts, or you can add a cherry (or two!) to your favorite beverage for a touch of delight.

MAKE IT YOUR OWN

You can expect an approximate yield of 2 32-ounce jars per every 3 ¼ pounds of cherries. I encourage you to can as many cherries as you envision using or giving away. You can effortlessly scale this recipe by using this ratio. I also use a 2:1 ratio for my syrup: 2 cups of water per 1 cup of sugar. A heavy syrup can be used as well. To create a heavy syrup, use a 2:2 ratio: 2 cups of water per 2 cups of sugar.

INGREDIENTS

3 ¼ pounds cherries

3 cups water

1 ½ cups sugar

EQUIPMENT & TOOLS

2 32-ounce regular- or wide-mouth jars, rings, and lids

Water-boiling canning pot

Rack

Jar lifter

Saucepan

Thermometer

Strainer

Cherry pitter

Large pot

Measuring cups

Silicone spatula

Ladle

Wide-mouth funnel

Towel or drying rack

recipe continues

01 **Prepare your water-boiling canning pot.** Refer to Setting Up Your Water-Boiling Canning Pot on page 48.

02 **Ready your sterilized jars.** Once your canning pot has boiled for 5 minutes, remove the jars and rings. Remove lids from the saucepan. They're going to be hot to the touch, so use a jar lifter to protect your hands. Allow the jars, rings, and lids to cool.

03 **Rinse your cherries in cool water.**

04 **Prepare your cherries.** Begin by pulling the stem away from each cherry. Then, pit your cherries using a cherry pitter. Refer to How to Core Fruits and Vegetables on page 51.

05 **As you prepare your cherries, pack them into your jars.** Pack them as tightly and efficiently as possible.

06 **Prepare your syrup.** In your large pot, bring 3 cups of water and 1 ½ cups of sugar to a simmer. Use your spatula to continuously stir until the sugar has dissolved completely. Remove from heat.

07 **Transfer your syrup into your jars of cherries.** The syrup will be very hot, so do this carefully. Use your funnel to guide each pour, and use a ladle or measuring cup to transfer the syrup. Fill each jar to the lowest part of the jar's mouth, about ½ inch below the rim.

08 **Remove air bubbles.** If you see any bubbles in the jars, use a spatula to guide them out.

09 **Tidy up.** Wipe your jars clean, especially the rims, with a warm, damp towel.

10 **Add your lids and rings.** Tighten.

11 **Process your cherries.** Submerge your jars into your water-boiling canning pot. Allow them to boil for 25 minutes. Begin your timer once the water is boiling. Adjust for altitude if needed. Refer to The Science and Safety of Canning on page 36.

12 **Cool.** Carefully remove your jars from the water using a jar lifter, and set them on a towel or drying rack to cool.

13 **Ensure they have sealed.** Once cooled, either listen for your jar to "pop," an audible indication it has sealed, or push the center of the lid to see if it pops up and down. If it *doesn't*, it's sealed! Date your jar, and store for up to a year. If the lid *does* pop up and down, it did *not* seal. Simply put that jar in your refrigerator, and enjoy within a month.

CANNED MANDARINS

Steps: 13
Yield: Approximately 2 32-ounce jars

Canned Mandarins are *the* best way to quench a sweet craving without becoming overly full. After a savory meal, enjoy the light sweetness of these orange slices of joy.

MAKE
IT YOUR
OWN

You can expect an approximate yield of 2 32-ounce jars per every 3 ¾ pounds of mandarins. To achieve this yield, your mandarins must be packed efficiently. I also use a 2:1 ratio for my syrup: 2 cups of water per 1 cup of sugar. A heavy syrup can be used as well. To create a heavy syrup, use a 2:2 ratio: 2 cups of water per 2 cups of sugar.

INGREDIENTS

3 ¾ pounds mandarins

2 ½ cups water

1 ¼ cups sugar

EQUIPMENT & TOOLS

2 32-ounce regular- or wide-mouth jars, rings, and lids

Water-boiling canning pot

Rack

Jar lifter

Saucepan

Thermometer

Strainer

Large pot

Measuring cups

Silicone spatula

Ladle

Wide-mouth funnel

Towel or drying rack

recipe continues

01 **Prepare your water-boiling canning pot.** Refer to Setting Up Your Water-Boiling Canning Pot on page 48.

02 **Ready your sterilized jars.** Once your canning pot has boiled for 5 minutes, remove the jars and rings. Remove lids from the saucepan. They're going to be hot to the touch, so use a jar lifter to protect your hands. Allow the jars, rings, and lids to cool.

03 **Rinse your mandarins in cool water.**

04 **Prepare your mandarins.** Begin by peeling your mandarins. Discard or compost the peel, or rind, of each mandarin. Then, separate the individual segments of each mandarin. Finally, be sure to remove any loose or large pieces of inner (white) pith.

05 **As you prepare your mandarins, pack them into your jars.** Pack them as tightly and efficiently as possible.

06 **Prepare your syrup.** In your large pot, bring 2 ½ cups of water and 1 ¼ cups of sugar to a simmer. Use your spatula to continuously stir until the sugar has dissolved completely. Remove from heat.

07 **Transfer your syrup into your jars of mandarins.** Your syrup will be very hot, so do this carefully. Use your funnel to guide each pour, and use a ladle or measuring cup to transfer the syrup. Fill each jar to the lowest part of the jar's mouth, about ½ inch below the rim.

08 **Remove air bubbles.** If you see any bubbles in the jars, use a spatula to guide them out.

09 **Tidy up.** Wipe your jars clean, especially the rims, with a warm, damp towel.

10 **Add your lids and rings.** Tighten.

11 **Process your mandarins.** Submerge your jars into your water-boiling canning pot. Allow them to boil for 10 minutes. Begin your timer once your water is boiling. Adjust for altitude if needed. Refer to The Science and Safety of Canning on page 36.

12 **Cool.** Carefully remove the jars from the water using your jar lifter, and set them on a towel or drying rack to cool.

13 **Ensure they have sealed.** Once cooled, either listen for your jar to "pop," an audible indication it has sealed, or push the center of the lid to see if it pops up and down. If it *doesn't*, it's sealed! Date your jar, and store for up to a year. If the lid *does* pop up and down, it did *not* seal. Simply put that jar in your refrigerator, and enjoy within a month.

CANNED PEACHES

Steps: 18
Yield: Approximately 2 32-ounce jars

My sisters, Sarah and Amy, and I ate *hundreds* of Canned Peaches growing up. There were four treats we could count on eating when visiting my grandparents' farm: chocolate-covered peanuts, Aristocrat Pickles, Strawberry Jam, and *Canned Peaches*. My Grandma Trudy canned hundreds of peaches each season, and it seemed she was never in short supply. Most days, we ate them straight out of the jar.

Here in Nashville, I buy Georgia peaches from The Peach Truck and Tennessee peaches from Hancock Family Farm. Depending on how ripe the peaches are when I buy them, I often set them on my counter on a soft towel and cover them with a second soft towel for two to three days. They should feel squishy-but-not-too-squishy before you can them. They should be ripe but not bruised. *Ripeness matters.* Ripeness equals easy-to-peel skin which is essential for canning peaches that are smooth to the eye and touch. The more you can them, the more you'll get a feel for the level of ripeness you prefer before canning.

MAKE
IT YOUR
OWN

You can expect an approximate yield of 2 32-ounce jars per every 4 pounds of peaches. I encourage you to can as many peaches as you envision using or giving away. You can effortlessly scale this recipe by using this ratio. I also use a 2:1 ratio for my syrup: 2 cups of water per 1 cup of sugar. A heavy syrup can be used as well. To create a heavy syrup, use a 2:2 ratio: 2 cups of water per 2 cups of sugar.

INGREDIENTS

4 pounds peaches

20 cups water

3 teaspoons ascorbic acid

4 cups sugar

EQUIPMENT & TOOLS

2 32-ounce regular-mouth jars, rings, and lids

Water-boiling canning pot

Rack

Jar lifter

Saucepan

Thermometer

2 large bowls

Measuring cups and spoons

Strainer

Large pot

Slotted spoon

Cutting board

Knife

Silicone spatula

Ladle

Wide-mouth funnel

Small sieve

Towel or drying rack

recipe continues

01 **Prepare your water-boiling canning pot.** Refer to Setting Up Your Water-Boiling Canning Pot on page 48.

02 **Ready your sterilized jars.** Once your canning pot has boiled for 5 minutes, remove the jars and rings. Remove lids from the saucepan. They're going to be hot to the touch, so use a jar lifter to protect your hands. Allow the jars, rings, and lids to cool.

03 **Prepare your large bowl of acidic solution.** Fill your first large bowl with water and ascorbic acid: 1 cup of water per ¼ teaspoon of ascorbic acid. In total, I recommend using 12 cups of water and 3 teaspoons of ascorbic acid. This solution prevents your peaches from bruising or browning once they are peeled and cored.

04 **Rinse your peaches in cool water.**

05 **Blanch your peaches.** Fill a large pot with water, and bring to a boil. As you're waiting for the water to begin boiling, fill your second large bowl with ice water. (You can also plug your sink and fill it with ice water. Both the boiling water and ice water need to be ready at the same time.) Once the water is boiling, drop your peaches into the water for 90 seconds. Start timing after the last peach has been dropped. (Do *not* overcrowd your pot. Blanch a single layer of peaches at a time, and move through a couple rounds of blanching if needed.) After 90 seconds, use your slotted spoon to remove your peaches from the boiling water, and immediately submerge them in your ice water. Allow them to completely cool.

06 **While your peaches cool, wash and rinse the large pot you used to blanch them.** You can reuse this pot to prepare your syrup and cook your peaches.

07 **Peel your peaches.** Just as your boiling water was ready at the same time as your ice water, your acidic solution must be ready at the same time as this step. Using your hands, begin at the top, or stem, of your peach, and move toward the bottom, or tip. Immediately place the peach into your bowl of acidic solution. Keep your peaches here until you are ready to halve and core them.

08 **Halve and core your peaches.** Cut your peaches in half vertically. Then, remove the pit using your fingers. Refer to How to Core Fruits and Vegetables on page 51. Again, immediately place each peach into your bowl of acidic solution until your large pot of syrup is ready.

09 **Prepare your syrup.** In your large pot, bring 8 cups of water and 4 cups of sugar to a simmer. Use your spatula to continuously stir until the sugar has dissolved completely.

10 **Briefly cook your peaches.** Transfer your peaches to your large pot of syrup, and simmer for 5 minutes. The reason we simmer our peaches in a large pot of syrup rather than water alone is to prevent bruising or browning until they are in our jars and submerged in syrup.

11 **Pack your peaches.** Take a single halved peach at a time out of the syrup using a slotted spoon. Tightly pack your peaches into jars with each cavity facing downward. This helps prevent pockets of air inside the jars.

12 **Transfer your syrup into your jars of peaches.** Your syrup will be very hot, so do this carefully. Use your funnel to guide each pour, and use a ladle or a measuring cup to transfer your syrup. Fill each jar to the lowest part of the jar's mouth, about ½ inch below the rim. You may ladle your syrup over a small sieve for clearer syrup.

13   **Remove air bubbles.** If you see any bubbles in the jars, use a spatula to guide them out.

14   **Tidy up.** Wipe your jars clean, especially the rims, with a warm, damp towel.

15   **Add your lids and rings.** Tighten.

16   **Process your peaches.** Submerge your jars into your water-boiling canning pot. Allow them to boil for 30 minutes. Begin your timer once the water is boiling. Adjust for altitude if needed. Refer to The Science and Safety of Canning on page 36.

17   **Cool.** Carefully remove your jars from the water using a jar lifter, and set them on a towel or drying rack to cool.

18   **Ensure they have sealed.** Once cooled, either listen for your jar to "pop," an audible indication it has sealed, or push the center of the lid to see if it pops up and down. If it *doesn't*, it's sealed! Date your jar, and store for up to a year. If the lid *does* pop up and down, it did *not* seal. Simply put that jar in your refrigerator, and enjoy within a month.

CANNED PEARS

INGREDIENTS

4 pounds pears

20 cups water

3 teaspoons ascorbic acid

4 cups sugar

EQUIPMENT & TOOLS

2 32-ounce regular-mouth jars, rings, and lids

Water-boiling canning pot

Rack

Jar lifter

Saucepan

Thermometer

Large bowl

Measuring cups and spoons

Strainer

Vegetable peeler

Cutting board

Knife

Melon baller

Large pot

Slotted spoon

Silicone spatula

Ladle

Wide-mouth funnel

Small sieve

Towel or drying rack

recipe continues

Steps: 17
Yield: Approximately 2 32-ounce jars

My favorite running trail in Nashville is curtained by age-old vines that twist and grow straight into the blue sky. When I trained for my first-ever marathon in 2017, I ran this trail often. The more I ran, the more its vines took realistic shape. They imaginatively became the head of a golden retriever or a small car—just as the clouds above did as a child. There is a vine in the shape of a pear slightly over half-way through this trail. It was my signal that the toughest terrain was behind me. This vine became my target each time I ran. If I could make it to the pear-shaped vine with strength, I could finish my run with strength. By holding my head high, paying close attention to my surroundings, and using my imagination, a mundane, commonplace vine in the woods became a meaningful emblem, one to which I pay homage today any time I see it.

Pears, while inherently delicious, will forever remind me of this chapter of my life, a chapter full of early mornings chasing down a pear-shaped vine in the woods.

MAKE
IT YOUR
OWN

You can expect an approximate yield of 2 32-ounce jars per every 4 pounds of pears. I encourage you to can as many pears as you envision using or giving away. You can effortlessly scale this recipe by using this ratio. You can add 1 cinnamon stick to each 32-ounce jar for a touch of warmth and spice at Step 10. I also use a 2:1 ratio for my syrup: 2 cups of water per 1 cup of sugar. A heavy syrup can be used as well. To create a heavy syrup, use a 2:2 ratio: 2 cups of water per 2 cups of sugar. I recommend using Bartlett pears.

01 **Prepare your water-boiling canning pot.** Refer to Setting Up Your Water-Boiling Canning Pot on page 48.

02 **Ready your sterilized jars.** Once your canning pot has boiled for 5 minutes, remove the jars and rings. Remove lids from the saucepan. They're going to be hot to the touch, so use a jar lifter to protect your hands. Allow the jars, rings, and lids to cool.

03 **Prepare your large bowl of acidic solution.** Fill a large bowl with water and ascorbic acid: 1 cup of water per ¼ teaspoon of ascorbic acid. In total, I recommend using 12 cups of water and 3 teaspoons of ascorbic acid. This solution prevents your pears from bruising or browning once they are peeled and cored.

04 **Rinse your pears in cool water.**

05 **Pull or cut away the stems of your pears.**

06 **Peel your pears.** Carefully remove the skin from each pear using your vegetable peeler. If any part of the bottom-most point, or calyx, of the pear remains after peeling, cut it away. Immediately place each peeled pear into your bowl of acidic solution. Keep your pears here until you are ready to halve and core them.

07 **Halve and core your pears.** Cut your pears in half vertically. Then, remove the core using your melon baller. Refer to How to Core Fruits and Vegetables on page 51. Again, immediately place each pear into your bowl of acidic solution until your large pot of syrup is ready.

08 **Prepare your syrup.** In your large pot, bring 8 cups of water and 4 cups of sugar to a simmer. Use your spatula to continuously stir until the sugar has dissolved completely.

09 **Briefly cook your pears.** Transfer your pears to your large pot of syrup, and simmer for 5 minutes. The reason we simmer our pears in a large pot of syrup rather than water alone is to prevent bruising or browning until they are in our jars and submerged in syrup.

10 **Pack your pears.** Take a single halved pear at a time out of your syrup using your slotted spoon. Tightly pack your pears into your jars with each cavity facing downward. This helps prevent pockets of air inside the jars.

11 **Transfer your syrup into your jars of pears.** Your syrup will be very hot, so do this carefully. Use your funnel to guide each pour, and use a ladle or measuring cup to transfer your syrup. Fill each jar to the lowest part of jar's mouth, about ½ inch below the rim. You may ladle your syrup over a small sieve for clearer syrup.

12 **Remove air bubbles.** If you see any bubbles in the jars, use a spatula to guide them out.

13 **Tidy up.** Wipe your jars clean, especially the rims, with a warm, damp towel.

14 **Add your lids and rings.** Tighten.

15 **Process your pears.** Submerge your jars into your water-boiling canning pot. Allow them to boil for 25 minutes. Begin your timer once your water is boiling. Adjust for altitude if needed. Refer to The Science and Safety of Canning on page 36.

16 **Cool.** Carefully remove your jars from the water using your jar lifter, and set them on a towel or drying rack to cool.

17 **Ensure they have sealed.** Once cooled, either listen for your jar to "pop," an audible indication it has sealed, or push the center of the lid to see if it pops up and down. If it *doesn't*, it's sealed! Date your jar, and store for up to a year. If the lid *does* pop up and down, it did *not* seal. Simply put that jar in your refrigerator, and enjoy within a month.

CANNED PLUMS

Steps: 14
Yield: Approximately 2 32-ounce jars

When I daydream about creating our next home, I imagine incorporating the dynamic color palette of red plums. They are beautiful, aren't they? I envision covering the walls of a bedroom with Roman clay in muted orange—as if the wall itself is made of terracotta. The bed linens are earthy reds, desert pinks, and golden yellows. The curtains are light and complementary, and the floors remain simple and bare.

When we pay close attention, something as simple as a red plum can influence a daydream. When we examine the colors, smells, and tastes of fruits, they can teach us about ourselves and what speaks to us most. What comes to mind for you as you study the colors of a red plum?

MAKE
IT YOUR
OWN

You can expect an approximate yield of 2 32-ounce jars per every 4 pounds of plums. I encourage you to can as many plums as you envision using or giving away. You can effortlessly scale this recipe by using this ratio. I also use a 2:1 ratio for my syrup: 2 cups of water per 1 cup of sugar. A heavy syrup can be used as well. To create a heavy syrup, use a 2:2 ratio: 2 cups of water per 2 cups of sugar.

INGREDIENTS

4 pounds plums

8 cups water

4 cups sugar

EQUIPMENT & TOOLS

2 32-ounce regular-mouth jars, rings, and lids

Water-boiling canning pot

Rack

Jar lifter

Saucepan

Thermometer

Strainer

Cutting board

Knife

Large pot

Measuring cups

Silicone spatula

Slotted spoon

Ladle

Wide-mouth funnel

Small sieve

Towel or drying rack

recipe continues

01 **Prepare your water-boiling canning pot.** Refer to Setting Up Your Water-Boiling Canning Pot on page 48.

02 **Ready your sterilized jars.** Once your canning pot has boiled for 5 minutes, remove the jars and rings. Remove lids from the saucepan. They're going to be hot to the touch, so use a jar lifter to protect your hands. Allow the jars, rings, and lids to cool.

03 **Rinse your plums in cool water.**

04 **Halve and core your plums.** Cut your plums in half vertically. Then, remove the pit using your fingers. Refer to How to Core Fruits and Vegetables on page 51. Briefly set aside.

05 **Prepare your syrup.** In your large pot, bring 8 cups of water and 4 cups of sugar to a low boil. Use your spatula to continuously stir until the sugar has dissolved completely.

06 **Cook your plums.** Place your plums in your large pot of syrup, and boil for 1 minute. Then, reduce the heat to low, and allow plums to rest in syrup for 20 minutes.

07 **Pack your plums.** Take a single halved plum at a time out of your syrup using your slotted spoon. Tightly pack your plums into your jars with each cavity facing downward. This helps prevent pockets of air inside the jars.

08 **Transfer your syrup to your jars of plums.** The syrup will be very hot, so do this carefully. Use your funnel to guide each pour, and use a ladle or measuring cup to transfer your syrup. Fill each jar to the lowest part of the jar's mouth, about ½ inch below the rim. You may ladle your syrup over a small sieve for clearer syrup.

09 **Remove air bubbles.** If you see any bubbles in your jars, use a spatula to guide them out.

10 **Tidy up.** Wipe your jars clean, especially the rims, with a warm, damp towel.

11 **Add your lids and rings.** Tighten.

12 **Process your plums.** Submerge your jars into your water-boiling canning pot. Allow them to boil for 25 minutes. Begin your timer once your water is boiling. Adjust for altitude if needed. Refer to The Science and Safety of Canning on page 36.

13 **Cool.** Carefully remove your jars from the water using a jar lifter, and set them on a towel or drying rack to cool.

14 **Ensure they have sealed.** Once cooled, either listen for your jar to "pop," an audible indication it has sealed, or push the center of the lid to see if it pops up and down. If it *doesn't*, it's sealed! Date your jar, and store for up to a year. If the lid *does* pop up and down, it did *not* seal. Simply put that jar in your refrigerator, and enjoy within a month.

CANNED TOMATOES

Steps: 17
Yield: Approximately 2 32-ounce jars

Canned Tomatoes! Homemade chili, pasta, pizza, *and much more* can result from one 32-ounce jar of Canned Tomatoes. When I think of Canned Tomatoes, I think of Ohio, my childhood, and comfort food. In the introduction to this book, you can learn about Grandma Trudy's homemade chili, my favorite meal in the entire world, made from freshly-canned tomatoes grown in the Ohio countryside.

MAKE
IT YOUR
OWN

You can expect an approximate yield of 2 32-ounce jars per every 4 pounds of tomatoes. I encourage you to can as many tomatoes as you envision using or giving away. You can also substitute your lemon juice with citric acid. I recommend 2 tablespoons of lemon juice per 1 32-ounce jar, and you can substitute this with ½ teaspoon of citric acid to reduce its subtle notes of citrus.

INGREDIENTS

4 pounds tomatoes

4 tablespoons lemon juice

EQUIPMENT & TOOLS

2 32-ounce regular- or wide-mouth jars, rings, and lids

Water-boiling canning pot

Rack

Jar lifter

Saucepan

Thermometer

Measuring spoons

Strainer

Large pot

Large bowl

Cutting board

Knife

Slotted spoon

Ladle

Wide-mouth funnel

Small sieve

Silicone spatula

Towel or drying rack

recipe continues

01 **Prepare your water-boiling canning pot.** Refer to Setting Up Your Water-Boiling Canning Pot on page 48.

02 **Ready your sterilized jars.** Once your canning pot has boiled for 5 minutes, remove the jars and rings. Remove lids from the saucepan. They're going to be hot to the touch, so use a jar lifter to protect your hands. Allow the jars, rings, and lids to cool.

03 **Add 2 tablespoons of lemon juice to each jar.**

04 **Rinse your tomatoes in cool water.**

05 **Blanch your tomatoes.** Fill a large pot with water, and bring to a boil. As you're waiting for the water to begin boiling, fill a large bowl with ice water. (You can also plug your sink and fill it with ice water. Both the boiling water and ice water need to be ready at the same time.) Once the water is boiling, drop your tomatoes into the water for 60 seconds. Start timing after the last tomato has been dropped. (Do *not* overcrowd your pot. Blanch a single layer of tomatoes at a time, and move through a couple rounds of blanching if needed.) After 60 seconds, use your slotted spoon to remove your tomatoes from the boiling water, and immediately submerge them in your ice water. Allow them to completely cool.

06 **While your tomatoes cool, wash and rinse the large pot you used to blanch them.** You can reuse this pot to cook your tomatoes. Refill your large pot with water, and bring to a simmer.

07 **Core your tomatoes.** Use a paring knife. Refer to How to Core Fruits and Vegetables on page 51. Removing the core from your tomatoes will give you a starting point from which to begin peeling.

08 **Peel your tomatoes.** The thick skin of each tomato ought to easily peel away.

09 **Briefly cook your tomatoes.** Transfer your tomatoes to your large pot of water, and simmer for 5 minutes.

10 **Pack your tomatoes.** Take a single tomato at a time out of your water using your slotted spoon. Tightly pack your tomatoes into your jars.

11 **Transfer your water into your jars of tomatoes.** Your water will be very hot, so do this carefully. Use your funnel to guide each pour, and use a ladle or a measuring cup to transfer your water. Fill each jar to the lowest part of the jar's mouth, about ½ inch below the rim. You may ladle your water over a small sieve for clearer water.

12 **Remove air bubbles.** If you see any bubbles in the jars, use a spatula to guide them out.

13 **Tidy up.** Wipe your jars clean, especially the rims, with a warm, damp towel.

14 **Add your lids and rings.** Tighten.

15 **Process your tomatoes.** Submerge your jars into your water-boiling canning pot. Allow them to boil for 45 minutes. Begin your timer once your water is boiling. Adjust for altitude if needed. Refer to The Science and Safety of Canning on page 36.

16 **Cool.** Carefully remove your jars from the water using your jar lifter, and set them on a towel or drying rack to cool.

17 **Ensure they have sealed.** Once cooled, either listen for your jar to "pop," an audible indication it has sealed, or push the center of the lid to see if it pops up and down. If it *doesn't*, it's sealed! Date your jar, and store for up to a year. If the lid *does* pop up and down, it did *not* seal. Simply put that jar in your refrigerator, and enjoy within a month.

CANNED TOMATO JUICE

Steps: 19
Yield: Approximately 2 32-ounce jars

Canned Tomato Juice is exactly what you need to complement Canned Tomatoes. Each can be used separately, of course, but my favorite way to use them is together to make my favorite meal in the entire world, Grandma Trudy's homemade chili.

MAKE IT YOUR OWN

You can expect an approximate yield of 2 32-ounce jars per every 6–8 pounds of tomatoes. The reason there is a wide range is because tomatoes vary in terms of water content. I recommend beginning with 8 pounds. If you have extra tomato juice once you have filled 2 32-ounce jars, enjoy your surplus right away, or put it in your refrigerator, and enjoy within a week.

You can substitute your lemon juice with citric acid. I recommend 2 tablespoons of lemon juice per 1 32-ounce jar, and you can substitute this with ½ teaspoon of citric acid to reduce its subtle notes of citrus.

INGREDIENTS

8 pounds tomatoes

4 tablespoons lemon juice

EQUIPMENT & TOOLS

2 32-ounce regular- or wide-mouth jars, rings, and lids

Water-boiling canning pot

Rack

Jar lifter

Saucepan

Thermometer

Strainer

2 large pots

Large bowl

Slotted spoon

Cutting board

Knife

Potato masher

Ladle

Small sieve

Measuring spoons

Wide-mouth funnel

Towel or drying rack

recipe continues

01 **Prepare your water-boiling canning pot.** Refer to Setting Up Your Water-Boiling Canning Pot on page 48.

02 **Ready your sterilized jars.** Once your canning pot has boiled for 5 minutes, remove the jars and rings. Remove lids from the saucepan. They're going to be hot to the touch, so use a jar lifter to protect your hands. Allow the jars, rings, and lids to cool.

03 **Rinse your tomatoes in cool water.**

04 **Blanch your tomatoes.** Fill a large pot with water, and bring to a boil. As you're waiting for the water to begin boiling, fill your large bowl with ice water. (You can also plug your sink and fill it with ice water. Both the boiling water and ice water need to be ready at the same time.) Once the water is boiling, drop your tomatoes into the water for 60 seconds. Start timing after the last tomato has been dropped. (Do *not* overcrowd your pot. Blanch a single layer of tomatoes at a time, and move through a couple rounds of blanching if needed.) After 60 seconds, use your slotted spoon to remove your tomatoes from the boiling water, and immediately submerge them in your ice water. Allow them to completely cool.

05 **While your tomatoes cool, wash and rinse the large pot you used to blanch them.** You can reuse this pot to cook your tomatoes.

06 **Core your tomatoes.** Use a paring knife. Refer to How to Core Fruits and Vegetables on page 51. Removing the core from your tomatoes will give you a starting point from which to begin peeling.

07 **Peel your tomatoes.** The thick skin of each tomato ought to easily peel away.

08 **Cut your tomatoes into quarters.**

09 **Place your quartered tomatoes in your large pot.** Begin to heat your tomatoes on medium as you begin to crush them. Use a potato masher or large fork to crush your tomatoes for 10 minutes.

10 **Reduce heat, and boil on low for an additional 10 minutes.**

11 **Isolate your tomato juice.** Ladle your tomatoes out of your pot, and press them through a sieve or fine mesh strainer into your second large pot. (In place of a second large pot, you can also use a bowl, container, or blender to store your tomato juice as you isolate it. Ultimately, your tomato juice must be in a large pot at

Step 13.) You can use the bottom of your ladle or a flexible spatula to press your juice through your sieve or fine mesh strainer.

12 **Once you have isolated your tomato juice, add your lemon juice tablespoon by tablespoon.** Fully incorporate.

13 **Bring your tomato juice to a low boil for 1 minute.** Then, reduce heat, and simmer for a final 5 minutes.

14 **Transfer your tomato juice into your jars.** Your juice will be very hot, so do this carefully. Use your funnel to guide each pour, and use a ladle or a measuring cup to transfer your juice. Fill each jar to the lowest part of the jar's mouth, about ½ inch below the rim.

15 **Tidy up.** Wipe your jars clean, especially the rims, with a warm, damp towel.

16 **Add your lids and rings.** Tighten.

17 **Process your tomato juice.** Submerge your jars into your water-boiling canning pot. Allow them to boil for 40 minutes. Begin your timer once your water is boiling. Adjust for altitude if needed. Refer to The Science and Safety of Canning on page 36.

18 **Cool.** Carefully remove your jars from the water using a jar lifter, and set them on a towel or drying rack to cool.

19 **Ensure they have sealed.** Once cooled, either listen for your jar to "pop," an audible indication it has sealed, or push the center of the lid to see if it pops up and down. If it *doesn't*, it's sealed! Date your jar, and store for up to a year. If the lid *does* pop up and down, it did *not* seal. Simply put that jar in your refrigerator, and enjoy within a month.

CANNED TOMATO SAUCE

Steps: 21
Yield: Approximately 2 32-ounce jars

When you find yourself with a large bounty of freshly-grown tomatoes, Canned Tomato Sauce can be your go-to recipe. This recipe uses a large amount of tomatoes and results in a small yield. It also makes your home smell divine due to its long cooking time.

There is something romantic, cinematic even, about making our own tomato sauce. In our home, it means a delicious pasta dish is in our future. And, speaking of romanticism, one of my all-time favorite restaurants, Rolf and Daughters, specializes in homemade pasta and has a series of public playlists. I highly recommend playing one of their playlists while you create this recipe to set a tone that matches the smell, taste, and sight of this recipe.

INGREDIENTS

32 pounds tomatoes

4 tablespoons lemon juice

8 cloves garlic

¼ cup basil, finely chopped and loosely packed

2 teaspoons salt

EQUIPMENT & TOOLS

2 32-ounce regular- or wide-mouth jars, rings, and lids

Water-boiling canning pot

Rack

Jar lifter

Saucepan

Thermometer

Strainer

2 large pots

Large bowl

Slotted spoon

Cutting board

Knife

Potato masher

Ladle

Small sieve

Measuring spoons

Wide-mouth funnel

Towel or drying rack

recipe continues

It is crucial to fully grasp how tomato sauce is created to ultimately have a sauce that fits our personal preferences. Tomato sauce allows us to become artists in our kitchen. We can personalize its consistency, or viscosity, the herbs and spices we use, and ultimately, the way we incorporate it into our final dish.

Simply put, we take freshly-grown tomatoes and isolate their juice as if we are creating Canned Tomato Juice. Then, we evaporate, or boil off, the water content of that juice. Similar to how we boil jams and marmalades to thicken them, we boil tomato juice to thicken it significantly. The more water content we evaporate, the thicker our sauce will be.

This matters greatly when thinking about how you ultimately envision incorporating your sauce into your final dish. If you envision using it as a vegetarian sauce, you may want a thicker sauce. In other words, you may want to evaporate more of its water content. If you envision using it with added meat, you may want a thinner sauce. In other words, you may want to evaporate less of its water content.

This recipe intends to be a simple vegetarian sauce. It's thick enough to use alone. If you would like to add meat to your ultimate dish, I recommend reducing its boiling time by half, or one hour, at Step 15.

You can expect an approximate yield of 2 32-ounce jars per every 32 pounds of tomatoes. Similar to Canned Tomato Juice, yield may vary. This is because tomatoes vary in terms of water content. Keep a close eye on your sauce once you begin boiling it at Step 15, and remove it from heat as soon as it has reached your desired consistency.

You can substitute your lemon juice with citric acid. I recommend 2 tablespoons of lemon juice per 1 32-ounce jar, and you can substitute this with ½ teaspoon of citric acid to reduce its subtle notes of citrus. You can also add an extra ¼ cup of basil, finely chopped and loosely packed, for a more basil-forward flavor. Finally, I recommend adding at least ¼ cup of olive oil per 1 32-ounce jar when you're ready to use.

01 **Prepare your water-boiling canning pot.** Refer to Setting Up Your Water-Boiling Canning Pot on page 48.

02 **Ready your sterilized jars.** Once your canning pot has boiled for 5 minutes, remove the jars and rings. Remove lids from the saucepan. They're going to be hot to the touch, so use a jar lifter to protect your hands. Allow the jars, rings, and lids to cool.

03 **Rinse your tomatoes in cool water.**

04 **Blanch your tomatoes.** Fill a large pot with water, and bring to a boil. As you're waiting for the water to begin boiling, plug your sink, and fill it with ice water. Once the water is boiling, drop your tomatoes into the water for 60 seconds. Start timing after the last tomato has been dropped. (Do *not* overcrowd your pot. Blanch a single layer of tomatoes at a time, and move through a couple rounds of blanching if needed.) After 60 seconds, remove your tomatoes from the boiling water, and immediately submerge them in your ice water. Allow them to completely cool.

05 **While your tomatoes cool, wash and rinse the large pot you used to blanch them.** You can reuse this pot to cook your tomatoes.

06 **Core your tomatoes.** Use a paring knife. Refer to How to Core Fruits and Vegetables on page 51. Removing the core from your tomatoes will give you a starting point from which to begin peeling.

07 **Peel your tomatoes.** The thick skin of each tomato ought to easily peel away.

08 **Cut your tomatoes into quarters.**

09 **Place your quartered tomatoes in your large pot.** Begin to heat your tomatoes on medium as you begin to crush them. Use a potato masher or large fork to crush your tomatoes for 10 minutes.

10 **Reduce heat, and boil on low for an additional 10 minutes.**

11 **Isolate your tomato juice.** Ladle your tomatoes out of your pot, and press them through a sieve or fine mesh strainer into your second large pot. (In place of a second large pot, you can also use a bowl, container, or blender to store your tomato juice as you isolate it. Ultimately, your tomato juice must be in a large pot at Step 15.) You can use the bottom of your ladle or a flexible spatula to press your juice through your sieve or fine mesh strainer.

12 **Once you have isolated your tomato juice, add your lemon juice tablespoon by tablespoon.** Fully incorporate.

13 **Finely chop your garlic cloves, and add.** Fully incorporate.

14 **Add your basil and salt.** Fully incorporate.

15 **Bring your tomato sauce to a low boil for 2 hours.** Stir consistently. This is when a close eye, or your artistry, is required. Remember, this recipe intends to be a simple vegetarian sauce. If you would like to add meat to your ultimate dish, I recommend reducing the boiling time by half, or one hour, at this step.

16 **Once your tomato sauce has reached desired consistency, transfer it into your jars.** Your sauce will be very hot, so do this carefully. Use your funnel to guide each pour, and use a ladle or measuring cup to transfer your sauce. Fill each jar to the lowest part of the jar's mouth, about ½ inch below the rim.

17 **Tidy up.** Wipe your jars clean, especially the rims, with a warm, damp towel.

18 **Add your lids and rings.** Tighten.

19 **Process your tomato sauce.** Submerge your jars into your water-boiling canning pot. Allow them to boil for 40 minutes. Begin your timer once your water is boiling. Adjust for altitude if needed. Refer to The Science and Safety of Canning on page 36.

20 **Cool.** Carefully remove your jars from the water using your jar lifter, and set them on a towel or drying rack to cool.

21 **Ensure they have sealed.** Once cooled, either listen for your jar to "pop," an audible indication it has sealed, or push the center of the lid to see if it pops up and down. If it *doesn't*, it's sealed! Date your jar, and store for up to a year. If the lid *does* pop up and down, it did *not* seal. Simply put that jar in your refrigerator, and enjoy within a month.

PICKLING
RECIPES

Pickles! Pickles! *Pickles!*

What comes to mind when you read the words above? We often envision pickled cucumbers when we see the word *pickles* because it is the most ubiquitous pickle in the United States. Throughout the 1650s, more than a century before we declared independence from Great Britain, an industry of pickled cucumbers was born in present-day Brooklyn, New York. As European immigration increased and the use of dill became more popular, the production and consumption of pickles grew. Due to their safety and popularity, the United States Government rationed pickles during World War II and committed over 40 percent of all pickles to food for the armed forces (Pruitt 2019).

Historically and universally, our love for pickles is boundless. Today, we can create pickles from any fruit or vegetable. There is so much to love and appreciate about pickles. They are safe due to their acidic environment. (Refer to The Science and Safety of Canning **on page 36.**) They are easily customizable to our personal cravings and preferences, and they elevate any dish by adding a zippy and textured experience to every bite.

NOTES FOR PICKLING

Foundation

Before diving into your first pickling recipe, I encourage you to read the following sections of this book: Compare and Contrast: Canning, Pickling, and Preserving on page 34, The Science and Safety of Canning on page 36, and Routines, Tips, and Tricks on page 48, including How to Choose the Right Cucumbers to Pickle.

Preparation

Pickling, a category of canning that uses heat and acid to save fruits and vegetables for an extended period, results in bright, crunchy, and delightful additions to our meals. Remember, it is important to make sure your kitchen is a space in which you're ready to spend some time before making a pickling recipe. Refer to How to Use *The Wiley Canning Company Cookbook* on page 24.

Five of fifteen recipes in this chapter begin with setting up your water-boiling canning pot and sterilizing your jars, rings, and lids. Refer to Setting Up Your Water-Boiling Canning Pot on page 48. "Quick Pickles", or pickles that intend to be immediately stored in your refrigerator, provide accessibility to those who have minimal equipment or less preparation space.

Yield

Yield may vary. The following recipes ensure you will accomplish *at least* the yield provided. Three main factors affect final yield when pickling:

01 **The shape of our individual fruits and vegetables.** The shape may affect the way our fruits and vegetables spatially settle in our jars.

02 **The water content of our fruits and vegetables.** Ripe, well-hydrated fruits and vegetables may produce a slightly higher yield due to higher water content per fruit or vegetable.

03 **Our personal handling of our fruits and vegetables.** Pickling recipes can include whole, halved, quartered, or chopped fruits and vegetables. If we cut our fruits and vegetables into quarters, we may fit slightly less than if we fully chop them.

Acidification

Pickled fruits and vegetables are created by adding heat and acid. When an environment is highly acidic, bacterial growth is strongly inhibited. Refer to The Science and Safety of Canning on page 36. The acid, a vinegar, must be at least 5% acidic. If you experiment with custom or homemade vinegar, test the acidity, or pH, using pH strips.

Salt

It is important to use canning, or pickling, salt. Canning salt is made of sodium chloride (NaCl) and does *not* contain iodine. It is typically finely ground to increase its rate of solubility. In other words, it dissolves readily and evenly.

Storage

If a pickling recipe does not require a water-boiling canning pot, immediately store it in your refrigerator. If a pickling recipe *does* require a water-boiling canning pot, ensure your jars have properly sealed.

ARISTOCRAT PICKLES

Steps: 22
Yield: Approximately 3 16-ounce jars

Good things take time. This family-rooted, nostalgic, and delicious recipe requires seven days. Day 01 requires only three quick and easy steps: washing your cucumbers, slicing your cucumbers, and puttin' 'em in a container to soak for seven days.

Secondly, I do not process my Aristocrat Pickles in a water-boiling canning pot. I put them immediately in my refrigerator as my Grandma Trudy did. In hindsight, I realize she did this because we, her family, ate them so quickly. I quietly smile each time I think about our shared meals that included them as a key ingredient.

From this day forward, these must be eaten with barbecued chicken, beef, pork, jackfruit...*you name it!* Growing up, my Grandma Trudy served barbecued beef sandwiches and added one topping: Aristocrat Pickles. I rarely speak in absolutes, so I mean it when I say: their flavor complements every barbecue variety I have tried.

Finally, it's important to use pickling, or Kirby, cucumbers. Refer to How to Choose the Right Cucumbers to Pickle on page 52.

MAKE IT YOUR OWN

On Day 07, you can add an extra cinnamon stick for a touch of warmth and spice. You can also increase your celery seed, whole allspice, and whole cloves by up to ½ teaspoon. To store outside of your refrigerator, process in a water-boiling canning pot. Refer to Steps 01, 02, and 11-13 of Tangy Dill Pickles on Page 106.

INGREDIENTS

Day 01:

12 Kirby cucumbers (This is approximately 3 pounds.)

8 cups water

½ cup canning salt

Day 07:

10 ¾ cups water

1 teaspoon alum

1 teaspoon ground ginger

1 ⅔ cups apple cider vinegar

1 cup sugar

1 cinnamon stick

1 teaspoon celery seed

1 teaspoon whole allspice

1 teaspoon whole cloves

1 teaspoon canning salt

EQUIPMENT & TOOLS

1 128-ounce jar, ring, and lid or 1 gallon-size container and fitted lid

3 16-ounce regular- or wide-mouth jars, rings, and lids

Strainer

Cutting board

Knife

Large pot

Measuring cups and spoons

Silicone spatula

Ladle

Wide-mouth funnel

Towel

recipe continues

DAY 01:

01 **Rinse your cucumbers in cool water.**

02 **Prepare your cucumbers.** Cut away the top-most and bottom-most tips of each cucumber. Then, cut each cucumber horizontally, or into chips.

03 **Combine Day 01 ingredients.** Add your water (8 cups) and canning salt to your 128-ounce jar. Slowly stir until the salt has dissolved. Add your cucumber slices, and stir for 2-3 minutes. Loosely place your lid and ring on your jar.

04 **Soak for 7 days.** Stir for 2-3 minutes each day using your silicone spatula.

DAY 07:

05 **On Day 07, rinse your cucumber slices.** Pour them into your strainer, and rinse with cool water.

06 **Place your cucumbers in your large pot.** Add 5 cups of water.

07 **Add your alum, and fully incorporate.**

08 **Heat your cucumbers on low to medium for 10 minutes.** Use your spatula to slowly stir. Do not boil at this step.

09 **Drain your cucumbers.** Do not rinse. Return them to your large pot.

10 **Add 5 cups of water once more.**

11 **Add your ground ginger, and fully incorporate.**

12 **Heat your cucumbers on low to medium for 10 minutes.** Use your spatula to slowly stir. Do not boil at this step.

13 **Drain your cucumbers again.** Do not rinse. Return them to your large pot once more.

14 **Pickle your cucumbers.** Add your vinegar and ¾ cup water. Slowly stir.

15 **Add your sugar, and fully incorporate.**

16 **Add your cinnamon stick, celery seed, whole allspice, whole cloves, and salt.** Fully incorporate.

17 **Heat on low to medium for 30 minutes.** Do not boil.

18 **Transfer your pickles, including the brine and excluding the cinnamon stick, to your 16-ounce jars.** Your pickles will be very hot, so do this carefully. Use your funnel to guide you, and use a ladle or measuring cup to transfer your pickles. Fill each jar to the lowest part of the jar's mouth, about ½ inch below the rim.

19 **Remove air bubbles.** If you see any bubbles in the jars, use a spatula to guide them out.

20 **Tidy up.** Wipe your jars clean, especially the rims, with a warm, damp towel.

21 **Add your lids and rings.** Tighten.

22 **Date your jars, and store in your refrigerator.** Enjoy within a month.

TANGY DILL PICKLES

INGREDIENTS

12 Kirby cucumbers (This is approximately 3 pounds.)

2 ½ cups apple cider vinegar

1 cup water

2 teaspoons canning salt

Place in each jar:

1 small garlic clove, finely chopped

1 teaspoon dill seed

¼ teaspoon black pepper corn

¼ teaspoon mustard seed

⅛ teaspoon whole allspice

⅛ teaspoon alum

⅛ teaspoon ground mustard seed

⅛ teaspoon nutmeg

4 jar-length stalks fresh dill

EQUIPMENT & TOOLS

4 16-ounce wide-mouth jars, rings, and lids

Water-boiling canning pot

Rack

Jar lifter

Saucepan

Thermometer

Strainer

Cutting board

Knife

Measuring cups and spoons

Wooden spoon

Ladle

Wide-mouth funnel

Towel or drying rack

recipe continues

Steps: 13
Yield: Approximately 4 16-ounce jars

Tangy Dill Pickles is inspired by Grace Wiley, my great-grandmother. Look at her smile! Her scrunchie! Her *camera!* I was twenty-nine years old when I saw this photo for the first time. In a sense, it felt like looking in a mirror; the similarities are uncanny. So much of who we are is already within us— already a part of us—waiting patiently to be uncovered. This is my adaptation of her original recipe.

It's important to use pickling, or Kirby, cucumbers. Refer to How to Choose the Right Cucumbers to Pickle on page 52. Depending on the size of your individual cucumbers, you can fit 8-12 spears in each jar. I wrote this recipe to fit 12.

MAKE IT YOUR OWN
You can partially or fully substitute your dill seed with dill weed for a more dill-forward flavor. For a touch of added heat, you can add ⅛ teaspoon of red pepper flakes to each jar as well. Finally, if you prefer to reduce tanginess, partially or fully substitute your apple cider vinegar with white vinegar.

⟨ TANGY DILL PICKLES

01 **Prepare your water-boiling canning pot.** Refer to Setting Up Your Water-Boiling Canning Pot on page 48.

02 **Ready your sterilized jars.** Once your canning pot has boiled for 5 minutes, remove the jars and rings. Remove lids from the saucepan. They're going to be hot to the touch, so use a jar lifter to protect your hands. Allow the jars, rings, and lids to cool.

03 **Rinse your cucumbers in cool water.**

04 **Prepare your cucumbers.** Cut away the top-most and bottom-most tips of each cucumber. Then, cut each cucumber vertically into 4 even spears. Each cucumber must fit below the lowest part of the jar's mouth, about ½ below the rim. Briefly set aside.

05 **Place all ingredients in your jars.** Begin with your spices and herbs, and end with your cucumber spears. Depending on their size, you should be able to fit approximately 12 spears (3 cucumbers) into each jar.

06 **Prepare your brine.** Wash and rinse the saucepan you used to sterilize your lids. You can reuse this pan for your brine. Add your vinegar, water, and canning salt to your saucepan. Heat on low to medium until your salt has completely dissolved. Slowly stir using your wooden spoon. This may take 3 -5 minutes. Do not boil.

07 **Pickle your cucumbers.** Carefully pour or ladle your brine into your jars. Allow your funnel to assist you. Fill to the lowest part of the jar's mouth, about ½ inch below the rim. Make sure your brine completely covers your cucumber spears.

08 **Remove air bubbles.** If you see any bubbles in the jars, use a wooden spoon to guide them out.

09 **Tidy up.** Wipe your jars clean, especially the rims, with a warm, damp towel.

10 **Add your lids and rings.** Tighten.

11 **Process your pickles.** Submerge your jars into your water-boiling canning pot. Allow them to boil for 10 minutes. Begin your timer once your water is boiling. Adjust for altitude if needed. Refer to The Science and Safety of Canning on page 36.

12 **Cool.** Carefully remove your jars from the water using your jar lifter, and set them on a towel or drying rack to cool.

13 **Ensure they have sealed.** Once cooled, either listen for your jar to "pop," an audible indication it has sealed, or push the center of the lid to see if it pops up and down. If it *doesn't*, it's sealed! Date your jar, and store for up to a year. If the lid *does* pop up and down, it did *not* seal. Simply put that jar in your refrigerator, and enjoy within a month.

PICKLED BANANA PEPPERS

Steps: 10
Yield: 1 16-ounce jar

Pickled Banana Peppers are incredibly versatile. You can add them to salads, pizzas, sandwiches, soups, *and more*. You can also finely chop them and add them atop hummus and dips to enjoy with chips, crackers, and pita bread. Pickled Banana Peppers are a great way to incorporate peppers into your meals across generations, including children, because they are relatively mild and slightly sweet.

MAKE
IT YOUR
OWN
You can substitute your monk fruit sweetener with sugar or any sweetening agent, or omit it altogether. Two complementary additions include mustard seed or dried oregano. I recommend adding ⅛ teaspoon of each.

INGREDIENTS

½ pound banana peppers (This is approximately 3-4 banana peppers. Pepper size my vary.)

1 cup white vinegar

¼ cup water

½ teaspoon canning salt

⅓ teaspoon monk fruit sweetener

¾ teaspoon black peppercorns

1 garlic clove

EQUIPMENT & TOOLS

1 16-ounce regular- or wide-mouth jar, ring, and lid

Strainer

Cutting board

Knife

Saucepan

Measuring cups and spoons

Wooden spoon

Ladle

Wide-mouth funnel

Towel

recipe continues

01 **Rinse your peppers in cool water.**

02 **Prepare your peppers.** Slice the top and bottom, the stem and apex, away. Thinly slice each pepper horizontally to create small rings. Remove the inner pith and seeds.

03 **Pack your peppers.** Place the slices in your jar. Fill to the lowest part of the jar's mouth, about ½ inch below the rim.

04 **Finely chop your garlic clove.**

05 **Prepare your brine.** Add your vinegar, water, canning salt, monk fruit sweetener, black peppercorns, and garlic to your saucepan. Heat on low to medium until your salt and sweetener have completely dissolved. Slowly stir using your wooden spoon. This may take 3–5 minutes. Do not boil.

06 **Pickle your peppers.** Carefully pour or ladle your brine into your jar. Allow your funnel to assist you. Fill to the lowest part of the jar's mouth, about ½ inch below the rim. Make sure the brine completely covers your peppers. Use a wooden spoon to press your peppers down into the brine if needed.

07 **Remove air bubbles.** If you see any bubbles in the jar, use a wooden spoon to guide them out.

08 **Tidy up.** Wipe your jar clean, especially the rim, with a warm, damp towel.

09 **Add your lid and ring.** Tighten.

10 **Refrigerate.** Place the jar in your refrigerator to allow your peppers to pickle completely. Allow 24–48 hours before opening and enjoying.

PICKLED BEETS

Steps: 21
Yield: 1 32-ounce jar

Along with Canned Applesauce, Pickled Beets excite Sullivan. The deep purple of Pickled Beets adds sophistication and a colorful touch to any meal. My favorite way to enjoy Pickled Beets is to incorporate them into a variety of salads. You can create a rich salad with spinach, Pickled Beets, goat cheese, walnuts, and herbs, or you can add them to a nourishing garden salad. Finally, enjoying Pickled Beets with a soft cheese, such as stracciatella, burrata, ricotta, or goat cheese, feels whole in its simplicity. Generously add your favorite fresh herb (plus a dash of salt and pepper!) to this mix.

MAKE
IT YOUR
OWN

You can expect an approximate yield of 2 pounds of beets per every 1 32-ounce jar. I gravitate toward warmer spices when pickling beets, such as cinnamon and whole cloves. However, beets welcome a variety of spices and herbs depending on how you envision ultimately using them. I recommend the addition of mustard seed and fresh dill for a tangy and herbal end result. You can substitute your monk fruit sweetener with sugar or any sweetening agent, or you can omit it altogether.

INGREDIENTS

2 pounds whole beets

1 ¼ cups apple cider vinegar

¼ cup white vinegar

¼ cup water

¾ teaspoon canning salt

2 teaspoons monk fruit sweetener

1 bay leaf

½ cinnamon stick

5 whole cloves

EQUIPMENT & TOOLS

1 32-ounce regular- or wide-mouth jar, ring, and lid

Water-boiling canning pot

Rack

Jar lifter

Saucepan

Thermometer

Strainer

Vegetable brush

Cutting board

Knife

Large pot

Vegetable peeler

Measuring cups and spoons

Wooden spoon

Ladle

Wide-mouth funnel

Towel or drying rack

recipe continues

01 **Prepare your water-boiling canning pot.** Refer to Setting Up Your Water-Boiling Canning Pot on page 48.

02 **Ready your sterilized jar.** Once your water-boiling canning pot has boiled for 5 minutes, remove the jar and ring. Remove lid from the saucepan. They're going to be hot to the touch, so use your jar lifter to protect your hands. Allow jar, ring, and lid to cool.

03 **Wash your beets in cool water.** Rinse and scrub your beets using a vegetable brush.

04 **Trim your beets.** Cut away *part* of each stem, only the part that includes the leafy greens. Leave 1-2 inches of each stem in tact, as well as the root of each beet.

05 **Place your beets in a large pot.** Cover them completely with water. Bring to a low, gentle boil.

06 **Boil your beets for 30 minutes.** Ultimately, your beets should be soft enough to easily pierce with a toothpick or fork. If your beets are not thoroughly softened after 30 minutes, allow your beets to simmer for an additional 10 minutes, and test again.

07 **Once your beets are thoroughly softened, drain and rinse them.**

08 **Trim your beets once more.** Cut away the remaining stem and root of each beet.

09 **Peel your beets.** Carefully remove the skin from each beet using your vegetable peeler.

10 **Cut your beets.** Cut smaller beets into quarters, and cut larger beets into eighths.

11 **Pack your beets.** Place your beets in your jar, and add your cinnamon stick when you have filled your jar halfway. Fill to the lowest part of the jar's mouth, about ½ inch below the rim.

12 **Prepare the brine.** Add your vinegars, water, canning salt, monk fruit sweetener, bay leaf, and cloves to your saucepan. Heat on low to medium until your salt and sweetener have completely dissolved. Slowly stir using your wooden spoon. This may take 3–5 minutes. Do not boil.

13 **Briefly set aside your bay leaf.**

14 **Pickle your beets.** Carefully pour or ladle your brine into your jar. Allow your funnel to assist you. Fill to the lowest part of the jar's mouth, about ½ inch below the rim. Make sure your brine completely covers your beets. Use a wooden spoon to press your beets down into the brine if needed.

15 **Add your bay leaf.** You can slide your bay leaf down the side of your jar or set it on top of your pickled beets.

16 **Remove air bubbles.** If you see any bubbles in the jar, use a wooden spoon to guide them out.

17 **Tidy up.** Wipe your jar clean, especially the rim, with a warm, damp towel.

18 **Add your lid and ring.** Tighten.

19 **Process your beets.** Submerge your jar into your water-boiling canning pot. Allow it to boil for 30 minutes. Begin your timer once your water is boiling. Adjust for altitude if needed. Refer to The Science and Safety of Canning on page 36.

20 **Cool.** Carefully remove your jar from the water using a jar lifter, and set it on a towel or drying rack to cool.

21 **Ensure it has sealed.** Once cooled, either listen for your jar to "pop," an audible indication it has sealed, or push the center of the lid to see if it pops up and down. If it *doesn't*, it's sealed! Date your jar, and store for up to a year. If the lid *does* pop up and down, it did *not* seal. Simply put that jar in your refrigerator, and enjoy within a month.

PICKLED EGGS

Steps: 16
Yield: Approximately 3 16-ounce jars

There are two foods I can happily eat in surprising numbers in one sitting: Kumomoto oysters and Pickled Eggs. I very consciously limit myself when eating Pickled Eggs, but it's not due to a lack of craving. They are an all-time favorite snack and appetizer.

We begin this recipe by creating a pinhole in the large end of each egg. When you read The Science and Safety of Canning on page 36, you learned about the relationship between pressure and temperature. As we heat our eggs, or increase their temperature, we also increase their internal pressure. The air inside of each egg tries to escape due to this increased internal pressure. When we create a pinhole, we give the air a convenient opening from which to escape. If we do *not* make a pinhole, the air can still escape through microscopic pores in the egg's shell, but this may ultimately affect the shape of your boiled egg.

MAKE IT YOUR OWN

You can replace your whole cloves with a cinnamon stick. Simply cut one cinnamon stick into thirds and place ⅓ stick in each 16-ounce jar.

INGREDIENTS

12 eggs

1 small beet

2 cups apple cider vinegar

¾ cup beet juice

¼ cup sugar

1 ¾ teaspoons canning salt

9 whole cloves

EQUIPMENT & TOOLS

3 16-ounce wide-mouth jars, rings, and lids

Strainer

Vegetable brush

Cutting board

Knife

Vegetable peeler

Pin

Large pot with lid

Large bowl

Slotted spoon

Saucepan

Measuring cups and spoons

Wooden spoon

Ladle

Wide-mouth funnel

Towel

recipe continues

01 **Wash your beet in cool water.** Rinse and scrub your beet using a vegetable brush.

02 **Prepare your beet.** Cut away its leaves, stems, and root. Then, peel your beet using your vegetable peeler. Cut your peeled beet in half vertically. Cut each half in half vertically to create 4 pieces of beet. Finally, cut each fourth in half to ultimately create 8 pieces of beet. Briefly set aside.

03 **Prepare your eggs.** Create a pinhole at the large end of each egg.

04 **Gently place your eggs in your large pot.** Cover your eggs completely with water. There should be approximately 2 inches of water above your eggs.

05 **Add ¼ teaspoon canning salt.**

06 **Bring to a low to medium boil.** As soon as your water has reached its boiling point, turn your heat off completely, and place your lid on your large pot. Allow your eggs to rest for 12 minutes.

07 **Prepare your ice bath.** As your eggs are resting, fill a large bowl with ice water. (You can also plug your sink and fill it with ice water.)

08 **Once your eggs have rested for 12 minutes, use your slotted spoon to remove your eggs from your large pot.** Immediately submerge them in your ice bath. Allow them to completely cool.

09 **Once cooled, take a single egg at a time out of your ice bath to peel.** First, hold your egg under warm, gently-running water for 10–15 seconds. Then, gently crack its shell against a hard surface, such

as your countertop. Peel your egg under warm, gently-running water. This helps loosen the egg's shell without further cooking the egg and aids tremendously in the peeling process. Peel all your eggs.

10 **Once you've peeled your eggs, place 4 eggs in each jar.** Then, add your pieces of beet to each jar: place 3 pieces in your first jar, 3 pieces in your second, and 2 pieces in your third. Finally, add 3 whole cloves to each jar. Place your jars in your refrigerator while you prepare your brine.

11 **Prepare your brine.** Add your vinegar, beet juice, sugar, and 1½ teaspoons canning salt to your saucepan. Heat on low to medium until your sugar and salt have completely dissolved. Slowly stir using your wooden spoon. This may take 3–5 minutes. Do not boil.

12 **Pickle your eggs.** Once your brine is prepared, remove your jars from your refrigerator. Carefully pour or ladle your brine into your jars. Allow your funnel to assist you. Fill to the lowest part of each jar's mouth, about ½ inch below the rim.

13 **Remove air bubbles.** If you see any bubbles in the jars, use a wooden spoon to guide them out.

14 **Tidy up.** Wipe your jars clean, especially the rims, with a warm, damp towel.

15 **Add your lid and ring.** Tighten.

16 **Refrigerate.** Place the jars in your refrigerator to allow your eggs to pickle completely. Allow 24 hours before opening and enjoying. Enjoy within a week.

PICKLED GARLIC CLOVES

Steps: 15
Yield: 1 16-ounce jar

Pickled Garlic Cloves are a subtle yet powerful way to enliven any appetizer, entrée, or side. When I incorporate Pickled Garlic Cloves into salads, pastas, and roasted vegetables, I slice each pickled clove horizontally as thinly as I can into small sheets. When I use this recipe as an addition to hummus, I chop each pickled clove as finely as I can.

MAKE IT YOUR OWN

You can add 1 teaspoon of your favorite garlic-friendly herb, such as dried basil, dried oregano, dried parsley, or dried thyme, to your brine at Step 06. You can also substitute your monk fruit sweetener with sugar or any sweetening agent, or you can omit it altogether.

INGREDIENTS

6 heads of garlic (This is approximately 72 cloves of garlic.)

¾ cup white wine vinegar

¼ cup white vinegar

¼ cup water

½ teaspoon canning salt

¼ teaspoon monk fruit sweetener

1 bay leaf

½ teaspoon black peppercorns

⅓ teaspoon mustard seed

EQUIPMENT & TOOLS

1 16-ounce regular- or wide-mouth jar, ring, and lid

Water-boiling canning pot

Rack

Jar lifter

Saucepan

Thermometer

Cutting board

Knife

Measuring cups and spoons

Wooden spoon

Ladle

Wide-mouth funnel

Towel or drying rack

recipe continues

01 **Prepare your water-boiling canning pot.** Refer to Setting Up Your Water-Boiling Canning Pot on page 48.

02 **Ready your sterilized jar.** Once your canning pot has boiled for 5 minutes, remove the jar and ring. Remove lid from the saucepan. They're going to be hot to the touch, so use a jar lifter to protect your hands. Allow the jar, ring, and lid to cool.

03 **Prepare your garlic.** Separate the heads of your garlic to free each individual garlic clove.

04 **Peel your garlic cloves.** Peel away the skin by beginning at the top of each clove and peeling toward to bottom. I first slice away the tips to start the peeling process.

05 **Pack your garlic cloves.** Place your garlic in your jar. Fill to the lowest part of the jar's mouth, about ½ inch below the rim.

06 **Prepare your brine.** Add your vinegar, water, canning salt, monk fruit sweetener, bay leaf, black peppercorns, and mustard seed to your saucepan. Heat on low to medium until your salt and sweetener have completely dissolved. Slowly stir with your wooden spoon. This may take 3–5 minutes. Do not boil.

07 **Briefly set aside your bay leaf.**

08 **Pickle your garlic.** Carefully pour or ladle your brine into your jar. Allow your funnel to assist you. Fill to the lowest part of the jar's mouth, about ½ inch below the rim. Make sure your brine completely covers your garlic cloves. Use a wooden spoon to press your garlic cloves down into the brine if needed.

09 **Add your bay leaf.** You can slide your bay leaf down the side of your jar or set it on top of your pickled garlic.

10 **Remove air bubbles.** If you see any bubbles in the jar, use a wooden spoon to guide them out.

11 **Tidy up.** Wipe your jar clean, especially the rim, with a warm, damp towel.

12 **Add your lid and ring.** Tighten.

13 **Process your garlic cloves.** Submerge your jar into your water-boiling canning pot. Allow it to boil for 10 minutes. Begin your timer once your water is boiling. Adjust for altitude if needed. Refer to The Science and Safety of Canning on page 36.

14 **Cool.** Carefully remove your jar from the water using a jar lifter, and set it on a towel or drying rack to cool.

15 **Ensure it has sealed.** Once cooled, either listen for your jar to "pop," an audible indication it has sealed, or push the center of the lid to see if it pops up and down. If it *doesn't*, it's sealed! Date your jar, and store for up to a year. If the lid *does* pop up and down, it did *not* seal. Simply put that jar in your refrigerator, and enjoy within a month.

PICKLED GINGER

Steps: 17
Yield: 1 16-ounce jar

Outside of our home, I most often see pickled ginger served with sushi. It is intended to cleanse, or reset, our palates between different types of sushi for us to fully enjoy the delicate differences between the components and flavors of each bite. Overall, Pickled Ginger is a fantastic addition to any meal that includes multiple flavors, especially when seafood is included, to help us enjoy the individuality of each component and flavor of a dynamic meal. Additionally, Pickled Ginger can be finely chopped and added to a fresh salad. I recommend adding finely-chopped Pickled Ginger and fresh mint to a bed of crisp, green lettuces for a refreshing and restorative mid-day meal.

Next, this recipe asks us to peel ¾ pound of fresh ginger root. Rise to this unique and meditative challenge, and allow yourself to take the peeling process slowly. The amorphous shape of ginger root requires focus to peel, and the best way to approach this is patiently. Enjoy the cleansing scent of ginger root as you work your way through ¾ pound.

MAKE IT YOUR OWN

You can add 1 teaspoon of whole allspice or whole cloves for a touch of warmth. You can also substitute your monk fruit sweetener with sugar or any sweetening agent, or you can omit it altogether.

INGREDIENTS

¾ pound ginger root

2 ¼ cups water

¾ cup rice vinegar

¼ cup white wine vinegar

½ teaspoon canning salt

2 teaspoons monk fruit sweetener

EQUIPMENT & TOOLS

1 16-ounce regular- or wide-mouth jar, ring, and lid

Water-boiling canning pot

Rack

Jar lifter

Saucepan

Thermometer

Strainer

Vegetable peeler

Cutting board

Knife

Measuring cups and spoons

Wooden spoon

Ladle

Wide-mouth funnel

Towel or drying rack

recipe continues

01 **Prepare your water-boiling canning pot.** Refer to Setting Up Your Water-Boiling Canning Pot on page 48.

02 **Ready your sterilized jar.** Once your canning pot has boiled for 5 minutes, remove the jar and ring. Remove lid from the saucepan. They're going to be hot to the touch, so use a jar lifter to protect your hands. Allow the jar, ring, and lid to cool.

03 **Wash and rinse the saucepan you used to sterilize your lids.** You can reuse this pan to boil your ginger.

04 **Rinse your ginger in cool water.**

05 **Peel your ginger.** *Patience is key.* Simply take your time, and do your best to peel your ginger as cleanly as possible using your vegetable peeler. You may cut away smaller nodules and discard or compost them when needed.

06 **Slice your ginger.** Position your ginger to be sliced vertically. Although its shape is amorphous, identify its longer side, and slice your ginger as thinly as possible vertically.

07 **Place your peeled and sliced ginger in your saucepan.** Add 2 cups water, and bring your ginger to a low to medium boil. Boil for 15 minutes. Slowly stir using your wooden spoon.

08 **Rinse your ginger.** Once your ginger has boiled for 15 minutes, drain and rinse it.

09 **Pack your ginger.** Place your ginger in your jar. Fill to the lowest part of the jar's mouth, about ½ inch below the rim.

10 **Prepare your brine.** Add your vinegars, ¼ cup of water, canning salt, and monk fruit sweetener to your saucepan. Heat on low to medium until your salt and sweetener have completely dissolved. Slowly stir with your wooden spoon. This may take 3–5 minutes. Do not boil.

11 **Pickle your ginger.** Carefully pour or ladle your brine into your jar. Allow your funnel to assist you. Fill to the lowest part of the jar's mouth, about ½ inch below the rim. Make sure the brine completely covers your ginger. Use your wooden spoon to press your ginger down into your brine if needed.

12 **Remove air bubbles.** If you see any bubbles in the jar, use a wooden spoon to guide them out.

13 **Tidy up.** Wipe your jar clean, especially the rim, with a warm, damp towel.

14 **Add your lid and ring.** Tighten.

15 **Process your ginger.** Submerge your jar into your water-boiling canning pot. Allow it to boil for 15 minutes. Begin your timer once your water is boiling. Adjust for altitude if needed. Refer to The Science and Safety of Canning on page 36.

16 **Cool.** Carefully remove your jar from the water using your jar lifter, and set it on a towel or drying rack to cool.

17 **Ensure it has sealed.** Once cooled, either listen for your jar to "pop," an audible indication it has sealed, or push the center of the lid to see if it pops up and down. If it *doesn't*, it's sealed! Date your jar, and store for up to a year. If the lid *does* pop up and down, it did *not* seal. Simply put that jar in your refrigerator, and enjoy within a month.

PICKLED GREEN BEANS

Steps: 13
Yield: Approximately 4 16-ounce jars

My recipe for Pickled Green Beans is...*spicy!* The good news is you can tone the heat, or spiciness, up or down depending on your personal tolerance. As someone who adds hot sauce and fresh jalapeños to *nearly* everything, I prefer a high level of heat myself. We tend to treat our Pickled Green Beans as a snack or appetizer. They are a wonderful addition to a charcuterie board or relish tray.

MAKE IT YOUR OWN
Add an additional ¼ teaspoon of red pepper flakes or ⅛ teaspoon of ground cayenne pepper to create more heat. Remove ¼ teaspoon of red pepper flakes and the ground cayenne pepper all together to create less heat. You can also add up to two extra stalks of fresh dill to each jar for a more dill-forward flavor.

INGREDIENTS

2 pounds green beans

3 ½ cups apple cider vinegar

1 ½ cups water

1 tablespoon canning salt

Place in each jar:

1 small garlic clove, finely chopped

½ teaspoon red pepper flakes

1 teaspoon dill seed

⅛ teaspoon alum

⅛ teaspoon ground cayenne pepper

2 jar-length stalks fresh dill

EQUIPMENT & TOOLS

4 16-ounce wide-mouth jars, rings, and lids

Water-boiling canning pot

Rack

Jar lifter

Saucepan

Thermometer

Strainer

Cutting board

Knife

Measuring cups and spoons

Wooden spoon

Ladle

Wide-mouth funnel

Towel or drying rack

recipe continues

01 **Prepare your water-boiling canning pot.** Refer to Setting Up Your Water-Boiling Canning Pot on page 48.

02 **Ready your sterilized jars.** Once your canning pot has boiled for 5 minutes, remove the jars and rings. Remove lids from the saucepan. They're going to be hot to the touch, so use a jar lifter to protect your hands. Allow the jars, rings, and lids to cool.

03 **Rinse your beans in cool water.**

04 **Prepare your beans.** Trim the ends of each bean to fit below the lowest part of the jar's mouth, about ½ inch below the rim. Briefly set aside.

05 **Place all ingredients in your jars.** Begin with your spices and herbs, and end with your beans.

06 **Prepare your brine.** Add your vinegar, water, and canning salt to your saucepan. Heat on low to medium until your salt has completely dissolved. Slowly stir with your wooden spoon. This may take 3–5 minutes. Do not boil.

07 **Pickle your beans.** Carefully pour or ladle your brine into your jars. Allow your funnel to assist you. Fill to the lowest part of the jar's mouth, about ½ inch below the rim. Make sure your brine completely covers your beans. Use your wooden spoon to press your beans down into the brine if needed.

08 **Remove air bubbles.** If you see any bubbles in the jars, use a wooden spoon to guide them out.

09 **Tidy up.** Wipe your jars clean, especially the rims, with a warm, damp towel.

10 **Add your lids and rings.** Tighten.

11 **Process your beans.** Submerge your jars into your water-boiling canning pot. Allow them to boil for 5 minutes. Begin your timer once your water is boiling. Adjust for altitude if needed. Refer to The Science and Safety of Canning on page 36.

12 **Cool.** Carefully remove your jars from the water using your jar lifter, and set them on a towel or drying rack to cool.

13 **Ensure they have sealed.** Once cooled, either listen for your jar to "pop," an audible indication it has sealed, or push the center of the lid to see if it pops up and down. If it *doesn't*, it's sealed! Date your jar, and store for up to a year. If the lid *does* pop up and down, it did *not* seal. Simply put that jar in your refrigerator, and enjoy within a month.

PICKLED JALAPEÑO PEPPERS

Steps: 11
Yield: 1 16-ounce jar

Pickled Jalapeño Peppers add a lively punch to a variety of dishes: avocado toast, tacos, burgers, soups, *and more!* As my older sister, Sarah, would say, "These've got a kick to 'em!"

It helps to understand how to control for heat, or spiciness, before we pickle jalapeño peppers. To grow healthily and fully, they produce an oil called capsaicin, which acts as a natural defense mechanism. Capsaicin is produced and stored in the inner pith (the capsaicin glands and placenta) of the pepper. We are often advised to remove the seeds from our peppers to reduce their heat level, and this is because the seeds are also attached to the inner pith and are more heavily coated in capsaicin. The seeds themselves are not what produce a pepper's heat; they are simply in close proximity to the inner pith. Removing the inner pith *and* seeds will reduce heat levels.

Next, as jalapeño peppers ripen, they transition from green to red. Red peppers are older and more mature, so they've had *more* time to produce *more* capsaicin. Therefore, red jalapeño peppers may contain more heat than green.

MAKE IT YOUR OWN

If you wish to reduce heat levels, choose young, green jalapeño peppers, and remove their inner piths and seeds. To maximize heat levels, choose mature, red jalapeños, and include their inner piths and seeds.

You can substitute your monk fruit sweetener with sugar or any sweetening agent, or omit it altogether. You can also add up to 1 teaspoon of your favorite dried herb.

INGREDIENTS

½ pound jalapeño peppers (This is approximately 5 to 7 jalapeño peppers. Pepper size may vary.)

1 cup white vinegar

¼ cup water

1 tablespoon lime juice

1 small garlic clove

½ teaspoon canning salt

⅓ teaspoon monk fruit sweetener

EQUIPMENT & TOOLS

1 16-ounce regular- or wide-mouth jar, ring, and lid

Strainer

Cutting board

Knife

Saucepan

Measuring cups and spoons

Wooden spoon

Ladle

Wide-mouth funnel

Towel

recipe continues

01 **Rinse your peppers in cool water.**

02 **Prepare your peppers.** Slice the top and bottom, the stem and apex, away. Thinly slice each pepper horizontally to create small rings. Remove your preferred amount of inner membrane or seeds here.

03 **Pack your peppers.** Place your peppers in your jar. Fill to the lowest part of the jar's mouth, about ½ inch below the rim.

04 **Wash your hands.**

05 **Finely chop your garlic clove.**

06 **Prepare your brine.** Add your vinegar, water, garlic, lime juice, canning salt, and monk fruit sweetener to your saucepan. Heat on low to medium until your salt and sweetener have completely dissolved. Slowly stir using your wooden spoon. This may take 3–5 minutes. Do not boil.

07 **Pickle your peppers.** Carefully pour or ladle your brine into your jar. Allow your funnel to assist you. Fill to the lowest part of the jar's mouth, about ½ inch below the rim. Make sure your brine covers your peppers. Use your wooden spoon to press your peppers down into the brine if needed.

08 **Remove air bubbles.** If you see any bubbles in the jar, use a wooden spoon to guide them out.

09 **Tidy up.** Wipe your jar clean, especially the rim, with a warm, damp towel.

10 **Add your lid and ring.** Tighten.

11 **Refrigerate.** Place your jar in your refrigerator to allow your peppers to pickle completely. Allow 24–48 hours before opening and enjoying.

PICKLED ONIONS

Steps: 8
Yield: 1 16-ounce jar

Year-round, if you open our refrigerator, you'll find bright pink Pickled Onions. To name only a few dishes, we eat Pickled Onions atop avocado toast, omelets, tacos, burgers, soups, and roasted vegetables.

Scaling this recipe is simple. If you pickle a large onion instead of a small, grab a second 16-ounce jar, and make additional brine. You can make two separate rounds of brine, or exactly double the brine.

MAKE IT YOUR OWN

You can go wild with this recipe! Add a few slices of jalapeño pepper if you prefer some heat. You can also increase your lime juice by ½–1 tablespoon for a more lime-forward flavor, especially if it's taco night. You can substitute your monk fruit sweetener with sugar or any sweetening agent, or you can omit it altogether.

INGREDIENTS

1 small red onion

¾ cup white vinegar

¼ cup water

1 tablespoon lime juice

½ teaspoon canning salt

¼ teaspoon monk fruit sweetener

EQUIPMENT & TOOLS

1 16-ounce regular- or wide-mouth jar, ring, and lid

Cutting board

Knife

Saucepan

Measuring cups and spoons

Wooden spoon

Ladle

Wide-mouth funnel

Towel

recipe continues

01 **Prepare your onion.** Cut your onion in half from top to bottom, or stem to root. Slice the stem and root away, and remove the outermost layer. Thinly slice each half.

02 **Pack your onion.** Place your onion in your jar. Fill to the lowest part of the jar's mouth, about ½ inch below the rim.

03 **Prepare your brine.** Add your vinegar, water, lime juice, canning salt, and monk fruit sweetener to your saucepan. Heat on low to medium until your salt and sweetener have completely dissolved. Slowly stir using your wooden spoon. This may take 3–5 minutes. Do not boil.

04 **Pickle your onion.** Carefully pour or ladle your brine into your jar. Allow your funnel to assist you. Fill to the lowest part of the jar's mouth, about ½ inch below the rim. Make sure your brine completely covers your onion. Use a wooden spoon to press your onion down into the brine if needed.

05 **Remove air bubbles.** If you see any bubbles in the jar, use a wooden spoon to guide them out.

06 **Tidy up.** Wipe your jar clean, especially the rim, with a warm, damp towel.

07 **Add the lid and ring.** Tighten.

08 **Refrigerate.** Place the jar in your refrigerator to allow your onion to pickle completely. Wait 24–48 hours before opening and enjoying.

PICKLED RADICCHIO

Steps: 10
Yield: 1 32-ounce jar

One of my favorite parts of working closely with fruits and vegetables is the opportunity to study the characteristics and patterns of their anatomies. A peeled garlic clove is utterly smooth, as smooth as a river rock that's been polished by the water's movement for centuries. A single raspberry is imaginatively composed of several tiny raspberries. When you cut your radicchio in half at Step 01, take a moment to notice its beautiful pattern. Like red cabbage, it resembles a baobab tree or coral reef. What do *you* notice as you work closely with fruits and vegetables?

MAKE IT YOUR OWN

You can expect an approximate yield of 1 small head (or ¾ pound) of radicchio per 1 32-ounce jar. You can add 1 teaspoon of anise seed or dried basil for an added aromatic touch. You can also substitute your monk fruit sweetener with sugar or any sweetening agent, or you can omit it altogether.

INGREDIENTS

1 small head radicchio (This is approximately ¾ pound.)

1 ¾ cups white vinegar

½ cup red wine vinegar

¼ cup water

¾ teaspoon canning salt

½ teaspoon monk fruit sweetener

1 teaspoon fennel seed

EQUIPMENT & TOOLS

1 32-ounce regular- or wide-mouth jar, ring, and lid

Cutting board

Knife

Saucepan

Measuring cups and spoons

Wooden spoon

Ladle

Wide-mouth funnel

Towel

recipe continues

01 **Prepare your radicchio.** Cut your head of radicchio in half from top to bottom, or top to core. Remove the outermost layer of leaves. Remove the core of *each half* by making a triangular cut. You are now left with 2 halves, each with its outermost layer of leaves removed and a triangular cut-out where the core once was.

02 **Slice your radicchio.** Briefly set aside one half of your radicchio. Take the other half of your radicchio, and cut it in half *again* from top to bottom, top to triangular cut-out. You are now left with 2 quarters. Thinly slice each quarter vertically, or longways.

03 **Repeat Step 02 for the second half of the radicchio.**

04 **Pack your radicchio.** Place your radicchio in your jar. Fill to the lowest part of the jar's mouth, about ½ inch below the rim.

05 **Prepare your brine.** Add your vinegars, water, canning salt, monk fruit sweetener, and fennel seed to your saucepan. Heat on low to medium until your salt and sweetener have completely dissolved. Slowly stir with your wooden spoon. This may take 3–5 minutes. Do not boil.

06 **Pickle your radicchio.** Carefully pour or ladle your brine into your jar. Allow your funnel to assist you. Fill to the lowest part of the jar's mouth, about ½ inch below the rim. Make sure your brine completely covers your radicchio. Use a wooden spoon to press your radicchio into the brine if needed.

07 **Remove air bubbles.** If you see any bubbles in the jar, use a wooden spoon to guide them out.

08 **Tidy up.** Wipe your jar clean, especially the rim, with a warm, damp towel.

09 **Add your lid and ring.** Tighten.

10 **Refrigerate.** Place the jar in your refrigerator to allow your radicchio to pickle completely.

PICKLED RADISHES

Steps: 13
Yield: 1 16-ounce jar

Similar to Pickled Onions, Pickled Radishes add a vibrant and cheerful color to your refrigerator. My favorite way to eat Pickled Radishes is to add a single layer of them to chicken salad and tuna salad sandwiches. They are especially delicious atop breakfast foods as well, including breakfast tacos, avocado toast, and an omelet full of your favorite vegetables and cheeses.

MAKE
IT YOUR
OWN

You may add up to ¾ teaspoon of mustard seed to your Pickled Radishes. You can also substitute your monk fruit sweetener with sugar or any sweetening agent, or you can omit it altogether.

INGREDIENTS

¾ pound radishes (excluding leaves)

¾ cup white vinegar

¼ cup water

1 tablespoon lime juice

½ teaspoon canning salt

¼ teaspoon monk fruit sweetener

1 garlic clove

1 bay leaf

EQUIPMENT & TOOLS

1 16-ounce regular- or wide-mouth jar, ring, and lid

Cutting board

Knife

Strainer

Saucepan

Measuring cups and spoons

Wooden spoon

Ladle

Wide-mouth funnel

Towel

recipe continues

01 **Prepare your radishes.** First, pull or cut away only the leaves. You may leave the root intact. Then measure ¾ pound of radishes.

02 **Rinse your radishes in cool water.**

03 **Slice your radishes.** First, cut away the stem and root of each radish. Then, slice each radish horizontally as thinly as possible.

04 **Pack your radishes.** Place your radishes in your jar. Fill to the lowest part of the jar's mouth, about ½ inch below the rim.

05 **Finely chop your garlic clove.**

06 **Prepare your brine.** Add your vinegar, water, lime juice, canning salt, monk fruit sweetener, garlic, and bay leaf to your saucepan. Heat on low to medium until your salt and sweetener have completely dissolved. Slowly stir using your wooden spoon. This may take 3–5 minutes. Do not boil.

07 **Briefly set aside your bay leaf.**

08 **Pickle your radishes.** Carefully pour or ladle your brine into your jar. Allow your funnel to assist you. Fill to the lowest part of the jar's mouth, about ½ inch below the rim. Make sure your brine completely covers your radishes. Use a wooden spoon to press your radishes down into the brine if needed.

09 **Add your bay leaf.** You can slide your bay leaf down the side of your jar or set it on top of your picked radishes.

10 **Remove air bubbles.** If you see any bubbles in the jar, use a wooden spoon to guide them out.

11 **Tidy up.** Wipe your jar clean, especially the rim, with a warm, damp towel.

12 **Add your lid and ring.** Tighten.

13 **Refrigerate.** Place your jar in your refrigerator.

PICKLED SHREDDED CARROTS

Steps: 9
Yield: 1 32-ounce jar

I moved to Boston, Massachusetts after graduating from college. To this day, Boston holds such magic to me. (Perhaps this is because I lived through *only one* winter season there.) Not only is it the city where Jared, my husband, and I first lived together, but it is also the city where I met Grace and Kyuwon, two of my dearest friends. We each worked at the Center for Brain Science at Harvard University, and as our friendships grew, our shared lunches increased in both frequency and length. In the center of campus, a brisk five-minute walk from our laboratories, food trucks gathered each day. We often found ourselves standing in line amidst others our age who were hungry for research, education, and a delicious lunch.

My favorite food truck was Bon Me. It has since developed into a cavalry of trucks and brick and mortars. My order was always the same: The J.P. It is a flavorful and filling sandwich made with tofu, cilantro, cucumber, red onion, and *pickled shredded carrots*. I now crave Pickled Shredded Carrots when making sandwiches, salads, soups, *and more*.

MAKE IT YOUR OWN

You can increase the amount of ground ginger by 1 teaspoon, or you can add 1 teaspoon of freshly-grated ginger root for a more ginger-forward flavor. You can also substitute your monk fruit sweetener with sugar or any sweetening agent, or you can omit it altogether.

INGREDIENTS

1 10-ounce bag shredded carrots

1 cup white wine vinegar

1 cup rice vinegar

½ cup water

1 tablespoon lime juice

2 small garlic cloves

1 teaspoon ground ginger

¾ teaspoon canning salt

¾ teaspoon monk fruit sweetener

EQUIPMENT & TOOLS

1 32-ounce regular- or wide-mouth jar, ring, and lid

Strainer

Cutting board

Knife

Saucepan

Measuring cups and spoons

Wooden spoon

Ladle

Wide-mouth funnel

Towel

recipe continues

01 **Rinse your shredded carrots in cool water.**

02 **Pack your carrots.** Fill to the lowest part of the jar's mouth, about ½ inch below the rim.

03 **Finely chop your garlic cloves.**

04 **Prepare your brine.** Add your vinegars, water, lime juice, garlic, ground ginger, canning salt, and monk fruit sweetener to your saucepan. Heat on low to medium until your ground ginger, salt, and sweetener have completely dissolved. This may take 3–5 minutes. Do not boil.

05 **Pickle your carrots.** Carefully pour or ladle your brine into your jar. Fill to the lowest part of the jar's mouth, about ½ inch below the rim. Make sure your brine completely covers your carrots. Use your wooden spoon to press them down into your brine if needed.

06 **Remove air bubbles.** If you see any bubbles in the jar, use a wooden spoon to guide them out.

07 **Tidy up.** Wipe the jar clean, especially the rim, with a warm, damp towel.

08 **Add your lid and ring.** Tighten.

09 **Refrigerate.** Place your jar in the refrigerator to allow your carrots to pickle completely. Allow 24–48 hours before opening and enjoying.

PICKLED SHRIMP

with Chef Sean Brock

Steps: 14
Yield: Approximately 4 32-ounce jars

Before Wiley Canning Company was born, I had a strong vision to gather others around canned, pickled, and preserved food. I knew how much value and joy canning, pickling, and preserving added to my life, and I was itching to share this practice with others. Chef Sean Brock is one of the very first people with whom I shared my vision. Immediately, he understood. As someone who has invested tremendously in carrying forward traditions and stories through food, Sean agrees that canning, pickling, and preserving is a sacred way to carry forward recipes *and voices*. When I began to write *The Wiley Canning Company Cookbook*, I knew Sean had to be a part of it. It is an immense honor to have him as a part of this work. Not only do I deeply admire his work and mind, but I also admire his role as a partner to my beloved friend, Adi, and as a father to their precious children. The Brock family is a key piece of our puzzle here in Nashville.

Pickled Shrimp with Chef Sean Brock is one of *the* most fun recipes I have ever made. *Pickled Shrimp!* It is so unexpected, and yet, it feels *so right!* You can enjoy this recipe on its own, or you can add Pickled Shrimp to a summer soup or cooled pasta salad.

This recipe was created in collaboration with Chef Sean Brock.

MAKE IT YOUR OWN

To store Pickled Shrimp, you can use one large container or divide it equally among 4 32-ounce jars. If you choose to use one large container, it must be one gallon or larger. The size of your shrimp will ultimately influence your storage needs.

INGREDIENTS

20 large shrimp, peeled and deveined

3 cups lemon juice

3 cups lime juice

Zest of one lemon

Zest of one lime

3 cups orange juice

5 garlic cloves

5 celery ribs

2 medium-sized fennel bulbs

5 medium carrots

5 jalapeño peppers

1 medium onion

5 cups Bragg's apple cider vinegar

5 teaspoons black peppercorns

5 tablespoons fennel seed

5 tablespoons fennel pollen

5 teaspoons turmeric

5 teaspoons red pepper flakes

5 tablespoons celery seed

5 tablespoons mustard seed

EQUIPMENT & TOOLS

4 32-ounce regular- or wide-mouth jars, rings, and lids

Strainer

Microplane

Cutting board

Knife

Vegetable peeler

Large pot

Measuring cups and spoons

Wooden spoon

Ladle

Wide-mouth funnel

Towel

recipe continues

01 Rinse your lemon, lime, celery ribs, fennel bulbs, carrots, and peppers in cool water.

02 Zest your lemon and lime using a Microplane.

03 Peel and thinly slice your garlic cloves. Peel away the skin by beginning at the top of each clove and peeling toward the bottom. I first slice away the tips to start the peeling process. Then, thinly slice.

04 Thinly slice your celery ribs.

05 Thinly shave your fennel bulbs and carrots using a vegetable peeler.

06 Slice your peppers. Slice the top and bottom, the stem and apex, away. Thinly slice each pepper horizontally to create small rings.

07 Thinly slice your onion. Cut your onion in half from top to bottom, or stem to root. Slice the stem and root away, and remove the outermost layer. Thinly slice each half.

08 Place *all* ingredients except for your shrimp in a large pot. Bring to a simmer. Slowly stir using your wooden spoon.

09 Once your liquid is simmering, add your shrimp, and simmer for 7 minutes. Continue slowly stirring.

10 Transfer all contents to a large container, or divide evenly among 4 32-ounce jars.

11 Remove air bubbles. If you see any bubbles in the jars, use a wooden spoon to guide them out.

12 Tidy up. Wipe your container or jars clean, especially the rims, with a warm, damp towel.

13 If using jars, add your lids and rings. Tighten.

14 Refrigerate. Place your container or jars in your refrigerator to allow your shrimp to pickle completely. Wait 24 hours before opening, and enjoy within 5 days.

PICKLED SWEET PEPPERS

Steps: 9
Yield: 1 32-ounce jar

Pickled Sweet Peppers not only look beautiful and colorful in your refrigerator, but they also accompany a variety of dishes due to their mild flavor. Most often, we use Pickled Sweet Peppers in salads. I also finely chop them to use as a taco topping. I love to combine Pickled Sweet Peppers, Pickled Jalapeño Peppers, and Pickled Onions for tacos and taco bowls especially. They brighten any dish that welcomes them with their color palette alone.

MAKE
IT YOUR
OWN
You can add up to 1 teaspoon of your favorite dried herb, such as oregano or parsley. If you would like to add heat, or spiciness, to your Pickled Sweet Peppers, I recommend adding 1 teaspoon of red pepper flakes to your brine at Step 04.

INGREDIENTS

1 pound sweet peppers
(This is approximately
1 quart of sweet peppers.
Pepper size my vary.)

2 cups white vinegar

¼ cup water

¾ teaspoon canning salt

1 ½ teaspoons black peppercorns

EQUIPMENT & TOOLS

1 32-ounce regular- or wide-mouth jar, ring, and lid

Strainer

Cutting board

Knife

Saucepan

Measuring cups and spoons

Wooden spoon

Ladle

Wide-mouth funnel

Towel or drying rack

recipe continues

01 **Rinse your peppers in cool water.**

02 **Prepare your peppers.** Slice the top and bottom, the stem and apex, away. Thinly slice each pepper horizontally to create small rings. Remove the inner piths and seeds.

03 **Pack your peppers.** Place your peppers in your jar. Fill to the lowest part of the jar's mouth, about ½ inch below the rim.

04 **Prepare your brine.** Add your vinegar, water, canning salt, and black peppercorns to your saucepan. Heat on low to medium until your salt has completely dissolved. Slowly stir using your wooden spoon. This may take 3–5 minutes. Do not boil.

05 **Pickle your peppers.** Carefully pour or ladle your brine into your jar. Allow your funnel to assist you. Fill to the lowest part of the jar's mouth, about ½ inch below the rim. Make sure your brine completely covers your peppers. Use a wooden spoon to press your peppers down into your brine if needed.

06 **Remove air bubbles.** If you see any bubbles in the jar, use a wooden spoon to guide them out.

07 **Tidy up.** Wipe your jar clean, especially the rim, with a warm, damp towel.

08 **Add your lid and ring.** Tighten.

09 **Refrigerate.** Place the jar in your refrigerator to allow your peppers to pickle completely. Allow 24–48 hours before opening and enjoying.

PRESERVING RECIPES

As a child, I could identify the day of the week based solely on the contents of my lunchbox. My parents almost always grocery shopped on Sunday afternoons. This meant my highly-coveted Lunchables was in my lunchbox on Mondays. On Tuesdays and Wednesdays, I might discover a sandwich made of deli meat and cheese, and on Thursdays, I would inevitably find a peanut butter and Raspberry Jam sandwich. Although my peanut butter and Raspberry Jam sandwich signaled, "Fresh groceries are running low," I came to prefer Thursdays. I came to prefer the reliable, simple, and comforting flavor of that PB&J. And while it may have signaled that we were low on fresh groceries, it also signaled, "Tomorrow's Friday!" Fridays, of course, were reserved for pizza from the school cafeteria.

More than canned and pickled fruits and vegetables, preserved fruits and vegetables ignite nostalgia. The taste of Raspberry Jam immediately reminds me of my elementary school's fluorescently-lit cafeteria. It immediately reminds me of the fifteen cents I carefully carried in my change purse to buy a carton of chocolate milk each day. It immediately reminds me I am deeply loved. I am so deeply loved that my parents grocery shopped nearly every Sunday afternoon, packed my lunchbox for school each day, and gave me a change purse to carry my coins for milk. More than anything, you see, that PB&J signaled, "I love you," each Thursday. Preserves can provide more than a delicious ingredient. They can make others feel seen, heard, *and loved*. It's no coincidence that preserving recipes are my favorite recipes to make throughout each holiday season and for special events, such as weddings and baby showers.

NOTES FOR PRESERVING

Foundation

Before diving into your first preserving recipe, I encourage you to read the following sections of this book: Compare and Contrast: Canning, Pickling, and Preserving on page 34, The Science and Safety of Canning on page 36, Routines, Tips, and Tricks, particularly How to Core Fruits and Vegetables on page 51, How to Bathe Your Berries on page 52, and How to Detect the Setting Point of Jam and Marmalade on page 53.

Preparation

Preserving, a category of canning that uses heat and sugar to save a fruit or vegetable for an extended period, results in rich, aromatic scents that fill your home and colorful jars that fill your pantry. As always, it is important to make sure your kitchen is a space in which you're ready to spend some time before making a preserving recipe. Refer to How to Use *The Wiley Canning Company Cookbook* on page 24. Each recipe ahead begins with setting up your water-boiling canning pot and sterilizing your jars, rings, and lids. Refer to Setting Up Your Water-Boiling Canning Pot on page 48.

Yield

Yield may vary. The following recipes ensure you will accomplish *at least* the yield provided. Three main factors affect final yield when preserving:

01   **The water content of our fruits and vegetables.** Ripe, well-hydrated fruits and vegetables may produce a slightly higher yield due to higher water content per fruit or vegetable. Higher water content may affect your setting point as well, so pay close attention to both the drip test and freezer test when detecting the setting point of your jam or marmalade. Refer to How to Detect the Setting Point of Jam or Marmalade on page 53.

02   **Added pectin or sugar.** Using extra pectin or sugar to achieve a proper setting point may produce a higher yield.

03   **Boiling time.** If you add extra boiling time to achieve a proper setting point, it may produce a slightly lower yield.

Acidification

Most recipes ahead include lemon juice as an acidifier to increase safety. Refer to The Science and Safety of Canning on page 36.

Storage

Once your jars have properly sealed, I encourage you to remove your rings from your jars. Although this is not absolutely critical, there are three main reasons I encourage you to do so:

01   **You can reuse your rings for future recipes.**

02   **The removal of your rings will not affect the seals of your jars.** The lid is what creates a proper seal. Rings simply hold lids in place as they seal.

03   **You can easily see spoilage or bacterial growth inside jars once rings have been removed.**

APRICOT ALMOND JAM

Steps: 25
Yield: Approximately 5 8-ounce jars

Apricot Almond Jam offers a colorful and sweet addition to our toast, biscuits, desserts, *and more!* The use of almond extract elevates this jam and creates a dynamic, surprising, and delicious addition to our meal.

MAKE
IT YOUR
OWN

You can substitute your almond extract for a variety of nut extracts, including hazelnut, walnut, or macadamia nut extract.

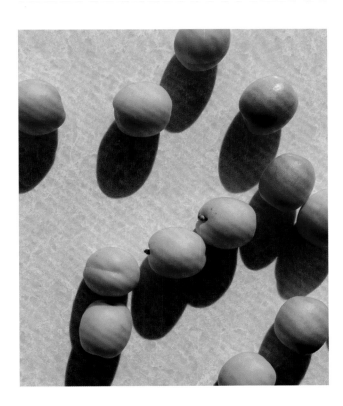

INGREDIENTS

3 pounds apricots

2 tablespoons lemon juice

2 tablespoons pectin

3 cups sugar

12 cups water

3 teaspoons ascorbic acid

1 teaspoon almond extract

EQUIPMENT & TOOLS

5 8-ounce jars, rings, and lids

Plate

Water-boiling canning pot

Rack

Jar lifter

Saucepan

Thermometer

2 large bowls

Measuring cups and spoons

Strainer

Large pot

Slotted Spoon

Cutting board

Knife

Potato masher

Silicone spatula

Splatter screen

Ladle

Wide-mouth funnel

Towel or drying rack

recipe continues

01 **Place a plate in your freezer.** This chilled plate comes in handy at Step 18 when ensuring your jam has set and is ready to be ladled into your jars.

02 **Prepare your water-boiling canning pot.** Refer to Setting Up Your Water-Boiling Canning Pot on page 48.

03 **Ready your sterilized jars.** Once your canning pot has boiled for 5 minutes, remove the jars and rings. Remove lids from the saucepan. They're going to be hot to the touch, so use a jar lifter to protect your hands. Allow the jars, rings, and lids to cool.

04 **Prepare a large bowl of acidic solution.** Fill your first large bowl with water and ascorbic acid: 1 cup of water per ¼ teaspoon of ascorbic acid. In total, I recommend using 12 cups of water and 3 teaspoons of ascorbic acid. This solution prevents your apricots from bruising or browning once they are peeled and cored.

05 **Rinse your apricots in cool water.**

06 **Blanch your apricots.** Fill a large pot with water, and bring to a boil. As you're waiting for the water to begin boiling, fill your second large bowl with ice water. (You can also plug your sink and fill it with ice water. Both the boiling water and ice water need to be ready at the same time.) Once the water is boiling, drop your apricots into the water for 90 seconds. Start timing after the last apricot has been dropped. (Do *not* overcrowd your pot. Blanch a single layer of apricots at a time, and move through a couple rounds of blanching if needed.) After 90 seconds, use your slotted spoon to remove your apricots from the boiling water, and immediately submerge them in your ice water. Allow them to completely cool.

07 **While your apricots cool, wash and rinse the large pot you used to blanch them.** You can reuse this pot to prepare your jam.

08 **Peel your apricots.** Just as your boiling water was ready at the same time as your ice water, your acidic solution must be ready at the same time as this step. Using your hands, begin at the top, or stem, of your apricot, and move toward the bottom, or tip. Immediately place the apricot into your bowl of acidic solution. Keep your apricots here until you are ready to halve and core them.

09 **Halve and core your apricots.** Cut your apricots in half vertically. Then, remove the pit. Refer to How to Core Fruits and Vegetables on page 51. Again, immediately place each peeled apricot into the bowl of acidic solution.

10 **Chop your apricots.** Chop each halved apricot into ½–1-inch pieces.

11 **Place your chopped apricots in your large pot.** Begin to heat your apricots on low to medium as you crush them. Use a potato masher or large fork to crush your apricots. I like to say I "semi-to-fully crush" my apricots. I allow small pieces of apricots to remain intact. Use your spatula to begin slowly stirring. This might take about 5–10 minutes. Do not boil.

12 **Add your lemon juice.** Once the apricots are crushed, continue slowly stirring. Add your lemon juice tablespoon by tablespoon. Include any jam that has made its way up the sides of your pot.

13 **Add your pectin.** As you continue stirring, add your pectin tablespoon by tablespoon. Include jam that has made its way up the sides of the pot.

14 **Add your sugar.** As you continue stirring, add your sugar cup by cup. Still include jam that has made its way up the sides of your pot.

15 **Boil your jam.** Increase heat to bring jam to a low, gentle boil. Boil for 10 minutes. Stir continuously. Use your splatter screen if needed.

16 **Add your almond extract.** Once your jam has boiled for 10 minutes, add your almond extract. Slowly stir, and fully incorporate.

17 **Remove any foam that has accumulated on the surface of your jam.**

18 **Make sure your jam has set.** Refer to How to Detect the Setting Point of Jam and Marmalade on page 53.

19 **Transfer your jam into jars.** Your jam will be very hot, so do this carefully. Use your funnel to guide each pour, and use a ladle or a measuring cup to transfer your jam. Fill each jar to the lowest part of the jar's mouth, about ½ inch below the rim.

20 **Remove air bubbles.** If you see any bubbles in the jars, use a spatula to guide them out.

21 **Tidy up.** Wipe your jars clean, especially the rims, with a warm, damp towel.

22 **Add your lids and rings.** Tighten.

23 **Process your jam.** Submerge your jars into your water-boiling canning pot. Allow them to boil for 10 minutes. Begin your timer once your water is boiling. Adjust for altitude if needed. Refer to The Science and Safety of Canning on page 36.

24 **Cool.** Carefully remove your jars from the water using your jar lifter, and set them on a towel or drying rack to cool.

25 **Ensure they have sealed.** Once cooled, either listen for your jar to "pop," an audible indication it has sealed, or push the center of the lid to see if it pops up and down. If it *doesn't*, it's sealed! Date your jar, and store for up to a year. If the lid *does* pop up and down, it did *not* seal. Simply put that jar in your refrigerator, and enjoy within a month.

BLACKBERRY LAVENDER JAM

Steps: 19
Yield: Appoximately 6 8-ounce jars

This recipe encapsulates many favorites for me. The color, to start, is one of my very favorites. Its deep purples nearly indistinguishable from its deep reds, the sight of this recipe alone brings me comfort. The smell, soft berry and lavender, immediately reminds me of the quiet of summer: the short moments when you might be the first awake in your household, the fleeting seconds when your sole focus is the application of sunscreen on your arms and shoulders, and the beginning of a summer shower when every strand of hair becomes soaked with warm water at once. Finally, the taste, a pop of tartness and hug of lavender, creates a surprising experience as your jawbone simultaneously tingles and softens.

MAKE IT YOUR OWN

You can increase the amount of lavender extract, ½ teaspoon at a time, for a more lavender-forward flavor (*and smell!*). Taste your jam after each addition of ½ teaspoon of lavender extract. You can also use any extract that sounds delicious to you, such as vanilla extract, in addition to or in place of lavender extract.

INGREDIENTS:

4 pints blackberries (This is approximately 3 pounds.)

2 tablespoons lemon juice

1 ½ teaspoons lavender extract

4 tablespoons pectin

3 cups sugar

EQUIPMENT & TOOLS

6 8-ounce jars, rings, and lids

Plate

Water-boiling canning pot

Rack

Jar lifter

Saucepan

Thermometer

Large bowl

Strainer

Large pot

Potato masher

Silicone spatula

Measuring cups and spoons

Splatter screen

Ladle

Wide-mouth funnel

Towel or drying rack

recipe continues

01 **Place a plate in your freezer.** This chilled plate comes in handy at Step 12 when ensuring your jam has set and is ready to be ladled into your jars.

02 **Prepare your water-boiling canning pot.** Refer to Setting Up Your Water-Boiling Canning Pot on page 48.

03 **Ready your sterilized jars.** Once your canning pot has boiled for 5 minutes, remove the jars and rings. Remove lids from the saucepan. They're going to be hot to the touch, so use a jar lifter to protect your hands. Allow the jars, rings, and lids to cool.

04 **Bathe and rinse your blackberries.** Refer to Bathing Your Berries on page 52.

05 **Place your blackberries in your large pot.** Begin to heat your blackberries on low to medium as you begin to crush them. Use a potato masher or large fork to fully crush your berries. Take your time. Use your spatula to begin slowly stirring. This might take 5–10 minutes. Do not boil.

06 **Add *part of* your lavender extract and *all* your lemon juice.** Once the berries are fully crushed, continue slowly stirring. Add 1 teaspoon only of lavender extract and your lemon juice tablespoon by tablespoon. Include any jam that has made its way up the sides of your pot.

07 **Add your pectin.** As you continue stirring, add your pectin tablespoon by tablespoon. Still include any jam that has made its way up the sides of the pot.

08   **Add your sugar.** As you continue stirring, add your sugar cup by cup. Still include any jam that has made its way up the sides of your pot.

09   **Boil your jam.** Increase heat to bring jam to a low, gentle boil. Boil for 10 minutes. Stir continuously. Use your splatter screen if needed.

10   **Add your remaining lavender extract.** Once your jam has boiled for 10 minutes, add your final ½ teaspoon of lavender extract. Slowly stir, and fully incorporate.

11   **Remove any foam that has accumulated on the surface of your jam.**

12   **Make sure your jam has set.** Refer to How to Detect the Setting Point of Jam and Marmalade on page 53.

13   **Transfer your jam into jars.** Your jam will be very hot, so do this carefully. Use your funnel to guide each pour, and use a ladle or a measuring cup to transfer your jam. Fill each jar to the lowest part of the jar's mouth, about ½ inch below the rim.

14   **Remove air bubbles.** If you see any bubbles in the jars, use a spatula to guide them out.

15   **Tidy up.** Wipe your jars clean, especially the rims, with a warm, damp towel.

16   **Add your lids and rings.** Tighten.

17   **Process your jam.** Submerge your jars into your water-boiling canning pot. Allow them to boil for 5 minutes. Begin your timer once your water is boiling. Adjust for altitude if needed. Refer to The Science and Safety of Canning on page 36.

18   **Cool.** Carefully remove your jars from the water using your jar lifter, and set them on a towel or drying rack to cool.

19   **Ensure they have sealed.** Once cooled, either listen for your jar to "pop," an audible indication it has sealed, or push the center of the lid to see if it pops up and down. If it *doesn't*, it's sealed! Date your jar, and store for up to a year. If the lid *does* pop up and down, it did *not* seal. Simply put that jar in your refrigerator, and enjoy within a month.

BLUEBERRY MINT JAM

Steps: 21
Yield: Approximately 6 8-ounce jars

This jam is both sweet *and* refreshing. This recipe is very special because it's the first preserving recipe I shared through Wiley Canning Company. My mom and I created it together in my Nashville home. The evening we created it, we served it warm with a freshly-baked peanut butter cookie and vanilla ice cream for dessert.

MAKE IT YOUR OWN
You can increase the amount of fresh mint by 1 tablespoon for a total of 3 tablespoons. You can also increase the amount of peppermint extract by ¼ teaspoon for a total of 1 teaspoon.

INGREDIENTS

4 pints blueberries (This is approximately 3 pounds.)

2 tablespoons fresh mint, finely chopped and loosely packed

2 tablespoons lemon juice

¾ teaspoon peppermint extract

4 tablespoons pectin

3 cups sugar

EQUIPMENT & TOOLS

6 8-ounce jars, rings, and lids

Plate

Water-boiling canning pot

Rack

Jar lifter

Saucepan

Thermometer

Large bowl

Strainer

Cutting board

Knife

Large pot

Potato masher

Silicone spatula

Measuring cups and spoons

Splatter screen

Ladle

Wide-mouth funnel

Towel or drying rack

recipe continues

01 **Place a plate in your freezer.** This chilled plate comes in handy at Step 14 when ensuring your jam has set and is ready to be ladled into your jars.

02 **Prepare your water-boiling canning pot.** Refer to Setting Up Your Water-Boiling Canning Pot on page 48.

03 **Ready your sterilized jars.** Once your canning pot has boiled for 5 minutes, remove the jars and rings. Remove lids from the saucepan. They're going to be hot to the touch, so use a jar lifter to protect your hands. Allow the jars, rings, and lids to cool.

04 **Bathe and rinse your blueberries.** Refer to Bathing Your Berries on page 52.

05 **Rinse your fresh mint.**

06 **Finely chop your fresh mint.** Briefly set aside.

07 **Place your blueberries in your large pot.** Begin to heat your blueberries on low to medium as you begin to crush them. Use a potato masher or large fork to fully crush your berries. Take your time. Use your spatula to begin slowly stirring. This might take 5–10 minutes. Do not boil.

08 **Add your fresh mint and lemon juice.** Once the berries are fully crushed, continue slowly stirring. Add your fresh mint and lemon juice tablespoon by tablespoon. Include any jam that has made its way up the sides of your pot.

09 **Add your pectin.** As you continue stirring, add your pectin tablespoon by tablespoon. Still include any jam that has made its way up the sides of your pot.

10 **Add your sugar.** As you continue stirring, add your sugar cup by cup. Still include any jam that has made its way up the sides of your pot.

11 **Boil your jam.** Increase heat to bring jam to a low, gentle boil. Boil for 10 minutes. Stir continuously. Use your splatter screen if needed.

12 **Add your mint extract.** Once your jam has boiled for 10 minutes, add your mint extract. Slowly stir, and fully incorporate.

13 **Remove any foam that has accumulated on the surface of your jam.**

14 **Make sure your jam has set.** Refer to How to Detect the Setting Point of Jam and Marmalade on page 53.

15 **Transfer your jam into jars.** Your jam will be very hot, so do this carefully. Use your funnel to guide each pour, and use a ladle or a measuring cup to transfer your jam. Fill each jar to the lowest part of the jar's mouth, about ½ inch below the rim.

16 **Remove air bubbles.** If you see any bubbles in the jars, use a spatula to guide them out.

17 **Tidy up.** Wipe your jars clean, especially the rims, with a warm, damp towel.

18 **Add your lids and rings.** Tighten.

19 **Process your jam.** Submerge your jars into your water-boiling canning pot. Allow them to boil for 5 minutes. Begin your timer once your water is boiling. Adjust for altitude if needed. Refer to The Science and Safety of Canning on page 36.

20 **Cool.** Carefully remove your jars from the water using your jar lifter, and set them on a towel or drying rack to cool.

21 **Ensure they have sealed.** Once cooled, either listen for your jar to "pop," an audible indication it has sealed, or push the center of the lid to see if it pops up and down. If it *doesn't*, it's sealed! Date your jar, and store for up to a year. If the lid *does* pop up and down, it did *not* seal. Simply put that jar in your refrigerator, and enjoy within a month.

FIG JAM

Steps: 20
Yield: Approximately 4 8-ounce jars

"It takes a village." I often hear this phrase regarding parenting. My goodness, it's the truth. I also felt a village around me as I wrote the words you are reading today. *The Wiley Canning Company Cookbook* feels like it's *ours* because of how much teamwork I felt as I brought it to life and as it, somehow, made it into your hands and homes.

This recipe was created when Jared's aunt, Aunt Beth, wrote me on a warm Sunday morning in August to tell me her fig tree was in bloom. I immediately drove to her house and picked fresh figs to create this jam. As you now make this jam, you will know it was created, tested, and enjoyed using figs grown right here in Nashville in Aunt Beth's backyard. Fig trees are one of the best trees to grow here in Nashville. They need bright light, and when in season, their beautiful figs need to be picked and eaten daily.

This jam is full of texture because I include the skin and seeds of the figs. I enjoy this jam with toast, cheese, or oatmeal.

MAKE IT YOUR OWN

Add a touch of ground cinnamon or cinnamon extract to honor the late summer season and welcome the new autumn season. I recommend adding ½ teaspoon at a time and taste testing after each addition.

INGREDIENTS

2 pounds figs

2 tablespoons lemon juice

3 tablespoons pectin

3 cups sugar

EQUIPMENT & TOOLS

4 8-ounce jars, rings, and lids

Plate

Water-boiling canning pot

Rack

Jar lifter

Saucepan

Thermometer

Strainer

Cutting board

Knife

Large pot

Silicone spatula

Potato masher

Measuring cups and spoons

Splatter screen

Ladle

Wide-mouth funnel

Towel or drying rack

recipe continues

01 **Place a plate in your freezer.** This chilled plate comes in handy at Step 13 when ensuring your jam has set and is ready to be ladled into your jars.

02 **Prepare a water-boiling canning pot.** Refer to Setting Up Your Water-Boiling Canning Pot for step-by-step photos on page 48.

03 **Ready your sterilized jars.** Once your canning pot has boiled for 5 minutes, remove the jars and rings. Remove lids from the saucepan. They're going to be hot to the touch, so use a jar lifter to protect your hands. Allow the jars, rings, and lids to cool.

04 **Rinse your figs in cool water.**

05 **Prepare your figs.** First, cut away the stems of your figs. Then, cut your figs in half vertically.

06 **Place your figs in your large pot.** Begin to heat your figs on low to medium as you stir them with your spatula. Slowly stir for 10 minutes. We simply want to warm and soften our figs.

07 **Crush your warmed figs.** Keep your heat on low to medium as you begin to crush them. Use a potato masher or large fork to fully crush your figs. Take your time. Make sure to crush all larger, fibrous pieces. You may see larger pieces of skin, and that is okay! Use your spatula to continue slowly stirring. This might take 5–10 minutes. Do not boil.

08 **Add your lemon juice.** Once the figs are crushed, continue slowly stirring. Add your lemon juice tablespoon by tablespoon. Include any jam that has made its way up the sides of your pot.

09 **Add your pectin.** As you continue stirring, add your pectin tablespoon by

tablespoon. Still include any jam that has made its way up the sides of your pot.

10 **Add your sugar.** As you continue stirring, add your sugar cup by cup. Still include any jam that has made its way up the sides of your pot.

11 **Boil your jam.** Increase heat to bring jam to a low, gentle boil. Boil for 5 minutes. Stir continuously. Use your splatter screen if needed.

12 **Remove any foam that has accumulated on the surface of your jam.**

13 **Make sure your jam has set.** Refer to How to Detect the Setting Point of Jam and Marmalade on page 53.

14 **Transfer your jam into jars.** Your jam will be very hot, so do this carefully. Use your funnel to guide each pour, and use a ladle or a measuring cup to transfer your jam. Fill each jar to the lowest part of the jar's mouth, about ½ inch below the rim.

15 **Remove air bubbles.** If you see any bubbles in the jars, use a spatula to guide them out.

16   **Tidy up.** Wipe your jars clean, especially the rims, with a warm, damp towel.

17   **Add your lids and rings.** Tighten.

18   **Process your jam.** Submerge your jars into your water-boiling canning pot. Allow them to boil for 10 minutes. Begin your timer once your water is boiling. Adjust for altitude if needed. Refer to The Science and Safety of Canning on page 36.

19   **Cool.** Carefully remove your jars from the water using your jar lifter, and set them on a towel or drying rack to cool.

20   **Ensure they have sealed.** Once cooled, either listen for your jar to "pop," an audible indication it has sealed, or push the center of the lid to see if it pops up and down. If it *doesn't*, it's sealed! Date your jar, and store for up to a year. If the lid *does* pop up and down, it did *not* seal. Simply put that jar in your refrigerator, and enjoy within a month.

MUSCADINE JAM

Steps: 21 steps
Yield: Approximately 4 8-ounce jars

Muscadine Jam is a unique and succulent jam to add to your pantry each year. Muscadines themselves are widely grown in the southeastern United States and are readily available at local farmers' markets in late summer here in Nashville, Tennessee.

This recipe is full of handwork and unique textures. Muscadine Jam asks us to separate its components, including the removal of up to five seeds per muscadine, before we blend, heat, and ultimately create a sweetened, spreadable product. This recipe allows us to enjoy and appreciate tactile work. Allow your hands to be messy and your kitchen to come alive.

MAKE IT YOUR OWN

I blend the skins and pulps of my muscadines using a blender at Step 07. They remain quite tough after the addition of heat if they are not finely chopped or blended. If you prefer a textured jam, you can blend your pulps and finely chop your skins instead of blending them together.

INGREDIENTS

2 pounds muscadines

2 tablespoons lemon juice

3 tablespoons pectin

3 cups sugar

EQUIPMENT & TOOLS

4 8-ounce jars, rings, and lids

Plate

Water-boiling canning pot

Rack

Jar lifter

Saucepan

Thermometer

Strainer

Cutting board

Knife

Blender

Large bowl

Large pot

Silicone spatula

Measuring cups and spoons

Splatter screen

Ladle

Wide-mouth funnel

Towel or drying rack

recipe continues

01 **Place a plate in your freezer.** This chilled plate comes in handy at Step 14 when ensuring your jam has set and is ready to be ladled into your jars.

02 **Prepare your water-boiling canning pot.** Refer to Setting Up Your Water-Boiling Canning Pot on page 48.

03 **Ready your sterilized jars.** Once your canning pot has boiled for 5 minutes, remove the jars and rings. Remove lids from the saucepan. They're going to be hot to the touch, so use a jar lifter to protect your hands. Allow the jars, rings, and lids to cool.

04 **Rinse your muscadines in cool water.**

05 **Prepare your muscadines.** First, cut your muscadines in half vertically. Then, separate the skin and pulp of each muscadine. The skin ought to easily peel away. Set skins in your blender, and set pulps in your large bowl.

06 **Remove the seeds from the pulp of each muscadine.** There are up to five seeds per muscadine. Add your seedless pulps to your blender.

07 **Blend skins and pulps until smooth.**

08 **Pour your blended muscadines into your large pot.** Begin to heat your muscadines

on low to medium. Use your spatula to begin slowly stirring. Do not boil.

09 **Add your lemon juice.** As you continue slowly stirring, add your lemon juice tablespoon by tablespoon. Include any jam that has made its way up the sides of your pot.

10 **Add your pectin.** As you continue stirring, add your pectin tablespoon by tablespoon. Still include any jam that has made its way up the sides of your pot.

11 **Add your sugar.** As you continue stirring, add your sugar cup by cup. Still include any jam that has made its way up the sides of your pot.

12 **Boil your jam.** Increase heat to bring jam to a low, gentle boil. Boil for 10 minutes. Stir continuously. Use your splatter screen if needed.

13 **Remove any foam that has accumulated on the surface of your jam.**

14 **Make sure your jam has set.** Refer to How to Detect the Setting Point of Jam and Marmalade on page 53.

15 **Transfer your jam into jars.** Your jam will be very hot, so do this carefully. Use your funnel to guide each pour, and use a ladle or a measuring cup to transfer your jam. Fill each jar to the lowest part of the jar's mouth, about ½ inch below the rim.

16 **Remove air bubbles.** If you see any bubbles in the jars, use a spatula to guide them out.

17 **Tidy up.** Wipe your jars clean, especially the rims, with a warm, damp towel.

18 **Add your lids and rings.** Tighten.

19 **Process your jam.** Submerge your jars into your water-boiling canning pot. Allow them to boil for 10 minutes. Begin your timer once your water is boiling. Adjust for altitude if needed. Refer to The Science and Safety of Canning on page 36.

20 **Cool.** Carefully remove your jars from the water using your jar lifter, and set them on a towel or drying rack to cool.

21 **Ensure they have sealed.** Once cooled, either listen for your jar to "pop," an audible indication it has sealed, or push the center of the lid to see if it pops up and down. If it *doesn't*, it's sealed! Date your jar, and store for up to a year. If the lid *does* pop up and down, it did *not* seal. Simply put that jar in your refrigerator, and enjoy within a month.

PEACH JAM

Steps: 24
Yield: Approximately 5 8-ounce jars

One of my favorite people in the world, my great aunt, lives in my home state of Ohio. Oftentimes when I visit her, I arrive to a beautiful, homemade dessert on her table. Two seats are immaculately set, each with an ornamental plate, a matching napkin, and a polished dessert fork. I once asked her, "Why do you do all of this *just* for me?" She responded with a piece of wisdom I carry with me to this day. She said, "We must create special experiences, especially when we're alone, to enjoy ourselves. We mustn't wait for a holiday or party to use our favorite plates or make homemade dessert. We can do these things for ourselves."

So, every once in a while, I buy expensive crackers and fancy cheese, and I pair them with Peach Jam to enjoy *alone*. I mustn't, after all, wait for a holiday or party to enjoy my favorite snack. What is one way you take care of yourself in this simple, special way? Allow your mind to wander as you create this recipe.

Here in Nashville, I buy Georgia peaches from The Peach Truck and Tennessee peaches from Hancock Family Farm. Depending on how ripe the peaches are when I buy them, I often set them on my counter on a soft towel and cover them with a second soft towel for two to three days. They should feel squishy-but-not-too-squishy before you preserve them. They should be ripe but not bruised.

**MAKE
IT YOUR
OWN**

Speaking of a holiday or party, you can add cinnamon or vanilla extract to this recipe for a touch of warmth and celebration. I recommend adding ½ teaspoon at a time and taste testing after each addition.

INGREDIENTS

3 pounds peaches

2 tablespoons lemon juice

4 tablespoons pectin

3 cups sugar

12 cups water

3 teaspoons ascorbic acid

EQUIPMENT & TOOLS

5 8-ounce jars, rings, and lids

Plate

Water-boiling canning pot

Rack

Jar lifter

Saucepan

Thermometer

2 large bowls

Measuring cups and spoons

Strainer

Large pot

Slotted Spoon

Cutting board

Knife

Potato masher

Silicone spatula

Splatter screen

Ladle

Wide-mouth funnel

Towel or drying rack

recipe continues

01 **Place a plate in your freezer.** This chilled plate comes in handy at Step 17 when ensuring your jam has set and is ready to be ladled into your jars.

02 **Prepare a water-boiling canning pot.** Refer to Setting Up Your Water-Boiling Canning Pot for step-by-step photos on page 48.

03 **Ready your sterilized jars.** Once your canning pot has boiled for 5 minutes, remove the jars and rings. Remove lids from the saucepan. They're going to be hot to the touch, so use a jar lifter to protect your hands. Allow the jars, rings, and lids to cool.

04 **Prepare a large bowl of acidic solution.** Fill your first large bowl with water and ascorbic acid: 1 cup of water per ¼ teaspoon of ascorbic acid. In total, I recommend using 12 cups of water and 3 teaspoons of ascorbic acid. This solution prevents your peaches from bruising or browning once they are peeled and cored.

05 **Rinse your peaches in cool water.**

06 **Blanch your peaches.** Fill a large pot with water, and bring to a boil. As you're waiting for the water to begin boiling, fill your second large bowl with ice water. (You can also plug your sink and fill it with ice water. Both the boiling water and ice water need to be ready at the same time.) Once the water is boiling, drop the peaches into the water for 90 seconds. Start timing after the last peach has been dropped. (Do *not* overcrowd the pot. Blanch a single layer of peaches at a time, and move through a couple rounds of blanching if needed.) After 90 seconds, use your slotted spoon to remove your peaches from the boiling water, and immediately submerge them in ice water. Allow them to cool completely.

07 **While your peaches cool, wash and rinse the large pot you used to blanch them.** You can reuse this pot to prepare your jam.

08 **Peel your peaches.** Just as your boiling water was ready at the same time as your ice water, your acidic solution must be ready at the same time as this step. Using your hands, begin at the top, or stem, of your peach, and move toward the bottom, or tip. Immediately place the peach into a bowl of acidic solution. Keep your peaches here until you are ready to halve and core them.

09 **Halve and core your peaches.** Cut your peaches in half vertically, and remove the pit. Again, immediately place each peeled peach into your bowl of acidic solution.

10 **Chop your peaches.** Chop each halved peach into ½–1-inch pieces in both length and width.

11 **Place your chopped peaches in your large pot.** Begin to heat your peaches on low to medium as you crush them. Use a potato masher or large fork to crush your peaches. I like to say I "semi-to-fully crush" my peaches. I allow small pieces of peaches to remain intact. Use your spatula to begin slowly stirring. This might take about 5–10 minutes. Do not boil.

12 **Add your lemon juice.** Once the peaches are crushed, continue slowly stirring. Add your lemon juice tablespoon by tablespoon. Include any jam that has made its way up the sides of your pot.

13 **Add your pectin.** As you continue stirring, add your pectin tablespoon by tablespoon. Still include any jam that has made its way up the sides of your pot.

14 **Add your sugar.** As you continue stirring, add your sugar cup by cup. Still include any jam that has made its way up the sides of your pot.

15 **Boil your jam.** Increase heat to bring jam to a low, gentle boil. Boil for 5 minutes. Stir continuously. Use your splatter screen if needed.

16 **Remove any foam that has accumulated on the surface of your jam.**

17 **Make sure your jam has set.** Refer to How to Detect the Setting Point of Jam and Marmalade on page 53.

18 **Transfer your jam into jars.** Your jam will be very hot, so do this carefully. Use your funnel to guide each pour, and use a ladle or a measuring cup to transfer your jam. Fill each jar to the lowest part of the jar's mouth, about ½ inch below the rim.

19 **Remove air bubbles.** If you see any bubbles in the jars, use a spatula to guide them out.

20 **Tidy up.** Wipe your jars clean, especially the rims, with a warm, damp towel.

21 **Add your lids and rings.** Tighten.

22 **Process your jam.** Submerge your jars into your water-boiling canning pot. Allow them to boil for 10 minutes. Begin your timer once your water is boiling. Adjust for altitude if needed. Refer to The Science and Safety of Canning on page 36.

23 **Cool.** Carefully remove jars from the water using your jar lifter, and set them on a towel or drying rack to cool.

24 **Ensure they have sealed.** Once cooled, either listen for your jar to "pop," an audible indication it has sealed, or push the center of the lid to see if it pops up and down. If it *doesn't*, it's sealed! Date your jar, and store for up to a year. If the lid *does* pop up and down, it did *not* seal. Simply put that jar in your refrigerator, and enjoy within a month.

PINEAPPLE
COCONUT JAM

Steps: 21
Yield: Approximately 4 8-ounce jars

Pineapple Coconut Jam transports me to a bare beach with Jared, Sullivan, and Jones, our golden retriever who *loves* to dig in the sand. The seagulls overhead are singing their ocean songs, and the marram grass holds more stories than I can imagine. This recipe tastes like a piña colada and *feels* like a well-earned vacation. This jam is a delightful addition to tacos and tostadas. It adds a tropical sweetness to the saltiness of warm tortillas filled with your favorite brisket, chicken, vegetables, and flavorful toppings. It is also, of course, delicious atop coconut-flavored treats, such as coconut ice cream or warm coconut cookies.

If you, like me, feel intimidated cutting pineapples at first, I assure you it will feel approachable and natural very quickly. I guide you through this process at Step 04.

MAKE IT YOUR OWN

You can increase or decrease the amount of coconut extract by ¼ teaspoon. I recommend using no more than 1 full teaspoon. A small amount goes a *long* way. And, because it's five o'clock somewhere, you can add *up to* 2 tablespoons of your favorite rum for a true piña colada jam. Do so after Step 11 once you've boiled your jam. Then, bring your jam to a low simmer for an additional 5 minutes.

INGREDIENTS

2 pounds freshly cut pineapple (This is about 2 small pineapples.)

¼ cup coconut water

2 tablespoons lemon juice

4 tablespoons pectin

3 cups sugar

2 tablespoons coconut flakes

¾ teaspoon coconut extract

EQUIPMENT & TOOLS

4 8-ounce jars, rings, and lids

Plate

Water-boiling canning pot

Rack

Jar lifter

Saucepan

Thermometer

Cutting board

Knife

Blender

Measuring cups and spoons

Large pot

Silicone spatula

Splatter screen

Ladle

Wide-mouth funnel

Towel or drying rack

recipe continues

01 **Place a plate in your freezer.** This chilled plate comes in handy at Step 14 when ensuring your jam has set and is ready to be ladled into your jars.

02 **Prepare your water-boiling canning pot.** Refer to Setting Up Your Water-Boiling Canning Pot on page 48.

03 **Ready your sterilized jars.** Once your canning pot has boiled for 5 minutes, remove the jars and rings. Remove lids from the saucepan. They're going to be hot to the touch, so use a jar lifter to protect your hands. Allow the jars, rings, and lids to cool.

04 **Prepare your pineapples.** First, cut away the top, or crown, of each pineapple. Then, cut away the bottom, or base. Stand the pineapple upright. Carefully slice away the prickly shell of the pineapple from top to bottom. Rotate the pineapple as you do. Eventually, you will have an upright pineapple with the top, bottom, and shell cut away. Once you do, slice your way around the core from top to bottom, cutting away as much juicy, fresh pineapple as possible. Finally, chop your fresh pineapple into 1–2-inch pieces in length and width. Repeat these steps to prepare your second pineapple.

05 **Place your chopped pineapple in your blender.** Add your coconut water. Blend until smooth.

06 **Pour your blended pineapple into your large pot.** Begin to heat your pineapple on low to medium. Use your spatula to begin slowly stirring. Do not boil.

07 **Add your coconut flakes.** As you continue stirring, add your coconut flakes tablespoon by tablespoon, and fully incorporate. Include any jam that has made its way up the sides of your pot.

08 **Add your lemon juice.** As you continue stirring, add your lemon juice tablespoon by tablespoon. Still include any jam that has made its way up the sides of your pot.

09 **Add your pectin.** As you continue stirring, add your pectin tablespoon by tablespoon. Still include any jam that has made its way up the sides of your pot.

10 **Add your sugar.** As you continue stirring, add your sugar cup by cup. Still include any jam that has made its way up the sides of your pot.

11 **Boil your jam.** Increase heat to bring jam to a low, gentle boil. Boil for 10 minutes. Stir continuously. Use your splatter screen if needed.

12 **Add your coconut extract.** Once your jam has boiled for 10 minutes, add your coconut extract. Slowly stir, and fully incorporate.

13 **Remove any foam that has accumulated on the surface of your jam.**

14 **Make sure your jam has set.** Refer to How to Detect the Setting Point of Jam and Marmalade on page 53.

15 **Transfer your jam into jars.** Your jam will be very hot, so do this carefully. Use your funnel to guide each pour, and use a ladle or a measuring cup to transfer your jam. Fill each jar to the lowest part of the jar's mouth, about ½ inch below the rim.

16 **Remove air bubbles.** If you see any bubbles in the jars, use a spatula to guide them out.

17 **Tidy up.** Wipe your jars clean, especially the rims, with a warm, damp towel.

18 **Add your lids and rings.** Tighten.

19 **Process your jam.** Submerge the jars into the water-boiling canning pot. Allow them to boil for 10 minutes. Begin your timer when the water begins boiling. Adjust for altitude if needed. Refer to The Science and Safety of Canning on page 36.

20 **Cool.** Carefully remove your jars from the water using your jar lifter, and set them on a towel or drying rack to cool.

21 **Ensure they have sealed.** Once cooled, either listen for your jar to "pop," an audible indication it has sealed, or push the center of the lid to see if it pops up and down. If it *doesn't*, it's sealed! Date your jar, and store for up to a year. If the lid *does* pop up and down, it did *not* seal. Simply put that jar in your refrigerator, and enjoy within a month.

RASPBERRY JAM

Steps: 18
Yield: Approximately 6 8-ounce jars

Raspberry Jam is a top-choice jam for me because of its texture alone. I enjoy the subtle crunch and added dimension of its seeds. I pair this jam with butter and bread, or I make a classic peanut butter and jam sandwich. You can also enjoy this jam atop yogurt, ice cream, *and more*. Enjoy it cool, at room temperature, or warm.

MAKE IT YOUR OWN

You can add any herb or extract of your choice, such as vanilla extract, for added complexity. I recommend adding ½ teaspoon at a time and taste testing after each addition.

INGREDIENTS

4 pints raspberries (This is approximately 3 pounds.)

2 tablespoons lemon juice

4 tablespoons pectin

3 cups sugar

EQUIPMENT & TOOLS

6 8-ounce jars, rings, and lids

Plate

Water-boiling canning pot

Rack

Jar lifter

Saucepan

Thermometer

Large bowl

Strainer

Large pot

Potato masher

Silicone spatula

Measuring cups and spoons

Splatter screen

Ladle

Wide-mouth funnel

Towel or drying rack

recipe continues

01 **Place a plate in your freezer.** This chilled plate comes in handy at Step 11 when ensuring your jam has set and is ready to be ladled into your jars.

02 **Prepare your water-boiling canning pot.** Refer to Setting Up Your Water-Boiling Canning Pot onn page 48.

03 **Ready your sterilized jars.** Once your canning pot has boiled for 5 minutes, remove the jars and rings. Remove lids from the saucepan. They're going to be hot to the touch, so use a jar lifter to protect your hands. Allow the jars, rings, and lids to cool.

04 **Bathe and rinse your raspberries.** Refer to Bathing Your Berries on page 52.

05 **Place your raspberries in your large pot.** Begin to heat your raspberries on low to medium as you begin to crush them. Use a potato masher or large fork to fully crush your berries. Take your time. Use your spatula to begin slowly stirring. This might take 5–10 minutes. Do not boil.

06 **Add your lemon juice.** Once the berries are fully crushed, continue slowly stirring. Add your lemon juice tablespoon by tablespoon. Include any jam that has made its way up the sides of your pot.

07　**Add your pectin.** As you continue stirring, add your pectin tablespoon by tablespoon. Still include any jam that has made its way up the sides of your pot.

08　**Add your sugar.** As you continue stirring, add your sugar cup by cup. Still include any jam that has made its way up the sides of your pot.

09　**Boil your jam.** Increase heat to bring jam to a low, gentle boil. Boil for 10 minutes. Stir continuously. Use your splatter screen if needed.

10　**Remove any foam that has accumulated on the surface of your jam.**

11　**Make sure your jam has set.** Refer to How to Detect the Setting Point of Jam and Marmalade on page 53.

12　**Transfer your jam into jars.** Your jam will be very hot, so do this carefully. Use your funnel to guide each pour, and use a ladle or a measuring cup to transfer your jam. Fill each jar to the lowest part of the jar's mouth, about ½ inch below the rim.

13　**Remove air bubbles.** If you see any bubbles in the jars, use a spatula to guide them out.

14　**Tidy up.** Wipe your jars clean, especially the rims, with a warm, damp towel.

15　**Add your lids and rings.** Tighten.

16　**Process your jam.** Submerge your jars into your water-boiling canning pot. Allow them to boil for 5 minutes. Begin your timer once your water is boiling. Adjust for altitude if needed. Refer to The Science and Safety of Canning on page 36.

17　**Cool.** Carefully remove your jars from the water using your jar lifter, and set them on a towel or drying rack to cool.

18　**Ensure they have sealed.** Once cooled, either listen for your jar to "pop," an audible indication it has sealed, or push the center of the lid to see if it pops up and down. If it *doesn't*, it's sealed! Date your jar, and store for up to a year. If the lid *does* pop up and down, it did *not* seal. Simply put that jar in your refrigerator, and enjoy within a month.

RED PEPPER JAM

Steps: 22
Yield: Approximately 3 8-ounce jars

Red Pepper Jam is a fantastic addition to a charcuterie board or warm bagel with cream cheese. It adds both spice and sweetness to the rich and salty flavors with which its paired, and this allows for a dynamic, unique sensory experience.

MAKE IT YOUR OWN

If you prefer more heat, or spiciness, you can add up to 1 extra teaspoon of red pepper flakes. This will result in a very spicy jam. You can also substitute the red pepper flakes with up to two jalapeño peppers and include part *or all* of their seeds. Refer to Make It Your Own under Pickled Jalapeño Peppers to learn more about capsaicin, a spicy oil produced by jalapeño peppers, and how to control its intensity when making a recipe.

INGREDIENTS

2 pounds red bell peppers

¾ cup red wine vinegar

1 ½ teaspoons red pepper flakes

2 tablespoons lemon juice

3 tablespoons pectin

2 cups sugar

EQUIPMENT & TOOLS

3 8-ounce jars, rings, and lids

Plate

Water-boiling canning pot

Rack

Jar lifter

Saucepan

Thermometer

Strainer

Cutting board

Knife

Blender

Measuring cups and spoons

Large pot

Silicone spatula

Splatter screen

Ladle

Wide-mouth funnel

Towel or drying rack

recipe continues

01 **Place a plate in your freezer.** This chilled plate comes in handy at Step 15 when ensuring your jam has set and is ready to be ladled into your jars.

02 **Prepare your water-boiling canning pot.** Refer to Setting Up Your Water-Boiling Canning Pot on page 48.

03 **Ready your sterilized jars.** Once your canning pot has boiled for 5 minutes, remove the jars and rings. Remove lids from the saucepan. They're going to be hot to the touch, so use a jar lifter to protect your hands. Allow the jars, rings, and lids to cool.

04 **Rinse your red peppers in cool water.**

05 **Cut your peppers.** Begin by cutting in a circular motion around the stem, or calyx, of each pepper. Completely remove the stem. Cut each pepper in half vertically, and remove its inner pith and seeds.

06 **Cut each half into quarters, then cut each quarter into ½–1-inch pieces in length.**

07 **Place your chopped peppers in your blender.** Add your red wine vinegar. Blend until smooth.

08 **Pour your blended peppers into your large pot.** Begin to heat your peppers on low to medium. Use your spatula to begin slowly stirring. Do not boil.

09 **Add your red pepper flakes.** As you continue stirring, add your red pepper flakes, and fully incorporate. Include any jam that has made its way up the sides of your pot.

10 **Add your lemon juice.** As you continue stirring, add your lemon juice tablespoon by tablespoon. Still include any jam that has made its way up the sides of your pot.

11 **Add your pectin.** As you continue stirring, add your pectin tablespoon by tablespoon. Still include any jam that has made its way up the sides of your pot.

12 **Add your sugar.** As you continue stirring, add your sugar cup by cup. Still include any jam that has made its way up the sides of your pot.

13 **Boil your jam.** Increase heat to bring jam to a low, gentle boil. Boil for 10 minutes. Stir continuously. Use your splatter screen if needed.

14 **Remove any foam that has accumulated on the surface of your jam.**

15 **Make sure your jam has set.** Refer to How to Detect the Setting Point of Jam and Marmalade on page 53.

16 **Transfer your jam into jars.** Your jam will be very hot, so do this carefully. Use your funnel to guide each pour, and use a ladle or a measuring cup to transfer your jam. Fill each jar to the lowest part of the jar's mouth, about ½ inch below the rim.

17 **Remove air bubbles.** If you see any bubbles in the jars, use a spatula to guide them out.

18 **Tidy up.** Wipe your jars clean, especially the rims, with a warm, damp towel.

19 **Add your lids and rings.** Tighten.

20 **Process your jam.** Submerge your jars into your water-boiling canning pot. Allow them to boil for 10 minutes. Begin your timer once your water is boiling. Adjust for altitude if needed. Refer to The Science and Safety of Canning on page 36.

21 **Cool.** Carefully remove your jars from the water using your jar lifter, and set them on a towel or drying rack to cool.

22 **Ensure they have sealed.** Once cooled, either listen for your jar to "pop," an audible indication it has sealed, or push the center of the lid to see if it pops up and down. If it *doesn't*, it's sealed! Date your jar, and store for up to a year. If the lid *does* pop up and down, it did *not* seal. Simply put that jar in your refrigerator, and enjoy within a month.

STRAWBERRY JAM

Steps: 19
Yield: Approximately 5 8-ounce jars

The readiness of strawberries signals the readiness of summer. The moment fresh strawberries are available at farmers' markets is the moment I know green, warm, and sunny days lie ahead.

It feels luxurious to bite into a strawberry only moments after it was picked. Although I could eat countless strawberries in their purest form, I often choose to turn them into smoothies, desserts, *and jam!*

MAKE
IT YOUR
OWN

If you feel drawn to add a touch of herbal goodness to this jam, I recommend adding up to ¾ teaspoon of rose water extract. Speaking of luxury, the combination of strawberry and rose water is both delicious and delicate. Add your rose water extract after you have boiled your jam at Step 11, and stir to fully incorporate.

INGREDIENTS

2 quarts strawberries (This is approximately 3 pounds.)

2 tablespoons lemon juice

4 tablespoons pectin

3 cups sugar

EQUIPMENT & TOOLS

5 8-ounce jars, rings, and lids

Plate

Water-boiling canning pot

Rack

Jar lifter

Saucepan

Thermometer

Large bowl

Strainer

Cutting board

Knife

Large pot

Potato masher

Silicone spatula

Measuring cups and spoons

Splatter screen

Ladle

Wide-mouth funnel

Towel or drying rack

recipe continues

01 **Place a plate in your freezer.** This chilled plate comes in handy at Step 12 when ensuring your jam has set and is ready to be ladled into your jars.

02 **Prepare your water-boiling canning pot.** Refer to Setting Up Your Water-Boiling Canning Pot on page 48.

03 **Ready your sterilized jars.** Once your canning pot has boiled for 5 minutes, remove the jars and rings. Remove lids from the saucepan. They're going to be hot to the touch, so use a jar lifter to protect your hands. Allow the jars, rings, and lids to cool.

04 **Bathe and rinse your strawberries.** Refer to Bathing Your Berries on page 52.

05 **Hull your strawberries.** In other words, remove the leafy cap, or calyx, from each strawberry.

06 **Rinse once more.**

07 **Place your strawberries in your large pot.** Begin to heat your strawberries on low to medium as you begin to crush them. Use a potato masher or large fork to fully crush your berries. Take your time. Use your spatula to begin slowly stirring. This might take 5–10 minutes. Do not boil.

08 **Add your lemon juice.** Once the berries are fully crushed, continue slowly stirring. Add your lemon juice tablespoon by tablespoon. Include any jam that has made its way up the sides of your pot.

09 **Add your pectin.** As you continue stirring, add your pectin tablespoon by tablespoon. Still include any jam that has made its way up the sides of your pot.

10 **Add your sugar.** As you continue stirring, add your sugar cup by cup. Still include any jam that has made its way up the sides of your pot.

11 **Boil your jam.** Increase heat to bring jam to a low, gentle boil. Boil for 10 minutes. Stir continuously. Use your splatter screen if needed.

12 **Make sure your jam has set.** Refer to How to Detect the Setting Point of Jam and Marmalade on page 53.

13 **Transfer your jam into jars.** Your jam will be very hot, so do this carefully. Use your funnel to guide each pour, and use a ladle or a measuring cup to transfer your jam. Fill each jar to the lowest part of the jar's mouth, about ½ inch below the rim.

14 **Remove air bubbles.** If you see any bubbles in the jars, use a spatula to guide them out.

15 **Tidy up.** Wipe your jars clean, especially the rims, with a warm, damp towel.

16 **Add your lids and rings.** Tighten.

17 **Process your jam.** Submerge your jars into your water-boiling canning pot. Allow them to boil for 5 minutes. Begin your timer once your water is boiling. Adjust for altitude if needed. Refer to The Science and Safety of Canning on page 36.

18 **Cool.** Carefully remove your jars from the water using your jar lifter, and set them on a towel or drying rack to cool.

19 **Ensure they have sealed.** Once cooled, either listen for your jar to "pop," an audible indication it has sealed, or push the center of the lid to see if it pops up and down. If it *doesn't*, it's sealed! Date your jar, and store for up to a year. If the lid *does* pop up and down, it did *not* seal. Simply put that jar in your refrigerator, and enjoy within a month.

SWEET AND SPICY PEACH JAM *with The Peach Truck*

Steps: 29
Yield: Approximately 5 8-ounce jars

Grandma Trudy raised us on Canned Peaches. She was no stranger to the feeling of holding a fresh peach, biting into it, and enjoying the classic taste of summertime each year. When Grandma Trudy was eighty-three years old, she ordered her first box of peaches from The Peach Truck. It was as though our worlds collided in a brand new way *through peaches!* It felt magical to enjoy *the same fruit* from *the same farm* from *the same people.*

Since 2012, it has been impossible to imagine summertime in Nashville without The Peach Truck. Now, as they've grown and stretched, it's hard to imagine summertime *nationwide* without them. The Peach Truck means a great deal to my family and me, so when the owners, Jessica and Stephen Rose, welcomed an opportunity to put our minds together, it felt like so much more than a recipe collaboration. Today, it honors a connection Grandma Trudy and I shared alongside, I'm sure, countless families across the country.

Refer to Peach Jam on Page 172 to learn more about the importance of ripeness before making this jam.

This recipe was created in collaboration with The Peach Truck.

MAKE IT YOUR OWN

If you wish to reduce heat levels as much as possible, choose young, green jalapeño peppers, and remove their inner piths and seeds at Step 05. Refer to Make It Your Own under Pickled Jalapeño Peppers to learn more about capsaicin, a spicy oil produced by jalapeño peppers, and how to control its intensity when making a recipe.

INGREDIENTS

3 pounds peaches

½ cup sweet peppers, finely chopped

¼ cup jalapeño peppers, finely chopped

2 tablespoons lemon juice

4 tablespoons pectin

3 cups sugar

12 cups water

3 teaspoons ascorbic acid

EQUIPMENT & TOOLS

5 8-ounce jars, rings, and lids

Plate

Water-boiling canning pot

Rack

Jar lifter

Saucepan

Thermometer

Cutting board

Knife

2 large bowls

Measuring cups and spoons

Strainer

Large pot

Slotted Spoon

Potato masher

Silicone spatula

Splatter screen

Ladle

Wide-mouth funnel

Towel or drying rack

recipe continues

01 **Place a plate in your freezer.** This chilled plate comes in handy at Step 22 when ensuring your jam has set and is ready to be ladled into your jars.

02 **Prepare your water-boiling canning pot.** Refer to Setting Up Your Water-Boiling Canning Pot on page 48.

03 **Ready your sterilized jars.** Once your canning pot has boiled for 5 minutes, remove the jars and rings. Remove lids from the saucepan. They're going to be hot to the touch, so use a jar lifter to protect your hands. Allow the jars, rings, and lids to cool.

04 **Prepare your sweet peppers.** Slice the top and bottom, the stem and apex, away. Thinly slice each pepper horizontally to create small rings. Remove the inner pith and seeds. Then, finely chop each small ring. Briefly set aside.

05 **Prepare your jalapeño peppers.** Slice the top and bottom, the stem and apex, away. Thinly slice each pepper horizontally to create small rings. Then, finely chop each small ring. Briefly set aside.

06 **Wash your hands.** You've just handled spicy peppers, so wash your hands to ensure you don't transfer their heat-containing oils anywhere unwanted.

07 **Prepare your large bowl of acidic solution.** Fill your first large bowl with water and ascorbic acid: 1 cup of water per ¼ teaspoon of ascorbic acid. In total, I recommend using 12 cups of water and 3 teaspoons of ascorbic acid. This solution prevents your peaches from bruising or browning once they are peeled and cored.

08 **Rinse your peaches in cool water.**

09 **Blanch your peaches.** Fill a large pot with water, and bring to a boil. As you're waiting for the water to begin boiling, fill your second large bowl with ice water. (You can also plug your sink and fill it with ice water. Both the boiling water and ice water need to be ready at the same time.) Once the water is boiling, drop your peaches into the water for 90 seconds. Start timing after the last peach has been dropped. (Do *not* overcrowd your pot. Blanch a single layer of peaches at a time, and move through a couple rounds of blanching if needed.) After 90 seconds, use your slotted spoon to remove your peaches from the boiling water, and immediately submerge them in your ice water. Allow them to completely cool.

10 **While your peaches cool, wash and rinse the large pot you used to blanch them.** You can reuse this pot to prepare your jam.

11 **Peel your peaches.** Just as your boiling water was ready at the same time as your ice water, your acidic solution must be ready at the same time as this step. Using your hands, begin at the top, or stem, of your peach, and move toward the bottom, or tip. Immediately place the peach into your bowl of acidic solution. Keep your peaches here until you are ready to halve and core them.

12 **Halve and core your peaches.** Cut your peaches in half vertically. Then, remove the pit. Refer to How to Core Fruits and Vegetables on page 51. Again, immediately place each peeled peach into your bowl of acidic solution.

13 **Chop your peaches.** Chop each halved peach into ½–1-inch pieces in both length and width.

14 **Place your chopped peaches in your large pot.** Begin to heat your peaches on low to medium as you crush them. Use a potato masher or large fork to crush your peaches. I like to say I "semi-to-fully crush" my peaches. I allow small pieces of peaches to remain intact. Use your spatula to begin slowly stirring. This should take about 5–10 minutes. Do not boil.

15 **Add your lemon juice.** Once the peaches are crushed, continue slowly stirring. Add your lemon juice tablespoon by tablespoon. Include any jam that has made its way up the sides of your pot.

16 **Add your pectin.** As you continue stirring, add your pectin tablespoon by tablespoon. Still include any jam that has made its way up the sides of your pot.

17 **Add your sugar.** As you continue stirring, add your sugar cup by cup. Still include any jam that has made its way up the sides of your pot.

18 **Add your sweet peppers, and continue stirring.**

19 **Add your jalapeño peppers, and continue stirring.**

20 **Boil your jam.** Increase heat to bring jam to a low, gentle boil. Boil for 5 minutes. Stir continuously. Use your splatter screen if needed.

21 **Remove any foam that has accumulated on the surface of your jam.**

22 **Make sure your jam has set.** Refer to How to Detect the Setting Point of Jam and Marmalade on page 53.

23 **Transfer your jam into jars.** Your jam will be very hot, so do this carefully. Use your funnel to guide each pour, and use a ladle or a measuring cup to transfer your jam. Fill each jar to the lowest part of the jar's mouth, about ½ inch below the rim.

24 **Remove air bubbles.** If you see any bubbles in the jars, use a spatula to guide them out.

25 **Tidy up.** Wipe your jars clean, especially the rims, with a warm, damp towel.

26 **Add your lids and rings.** Tighten.

27 **Process your jam.** Submerge your jars into your water-boiling canning pot. Allow them to boil for 10 minutes. Begin your timer once your water is boiling. Adjust for altitude if needed. Refer to The Science and Safety of Canning on page 36.

28 **Cool.** Carefully remove your jars from the water using your jar lifter, and set them on a towel or drying rack to cool.

29 **Ensure they have sealed.** Once cooled, either listen for your jar to "pop," an audible indication it has sealed, or push the center of the lid to see if it pops up and down. If it *doesn't*, it's sealed! Date your jar, and store for up to a year. If the lid *does* pop up and down, it did *not* seal. Simply put that jar in your refrigerator, and enjoy within a month.

CARA CARA ORANGE MARMALADE

with Chef Laura Lea Bryant

Steps: 24
Yield: Approximately 4 8-ounce jars

Friendships are one of the greatest fortunes of my life. My girlfriends and I plan time together as if it's as important as updating our driver's licenses or taking our children to doctor's appointments. This is because *it is*. I can't imagine motherhood, marriage, creativity, or love without 'em.

As I wrote this book, I pared my life down to the most essential. I reduced my exercise classes, shortened my runs, and stopped routinely visiting museums and parks. I became tunnel-visioned and lived more inwardly than outwardly. I couldn't bring myself, though, to completely pare down my time with girlfriends. We scheduled dinners, oftentimes months in advance, and looked forward to time together like a holiday. We are each other's keepers of our curiosities, joys, and heartaches. My conversations and time with them nourished my heart and mind as I brought this book to life.

Laura Lea Bryant is one of these girlfriends. Without fail, she encourages and supports me, no matter where my work leads me. Laura Lea is a renowned chef and food writer. She has written multiple cookbooks, and to have her as a part of this book is a fortune atop fortunes.

This recipe was created in collaboration with Chef Laura Lea Bryant.

MAKE IT YOUR OWN

You can substitute your Cara Cara oranges with Valencia or Seville oranges. It's important to use white chia seeds due to color alone. Black chia seeds will alter the color to a grayish tone.

INGREDIENTS

2 pounds Cara Cara oranges

3 cups water

2 tablespoons lemon juice

1 cup sugar or granulated monk fruit sweetener

2 teaspoons vanilla bean paste

⅓ cup white chia seeds

EQUIPMENT & TOOLS

4 8-ounce jars, rings, and lids

Plate

Water-boiling canning pot

Rack

Jar lifter

Saucepan

Thermometer

Strainer

Cutting board

Knife

Large bowl

Blender

Large pot

Measuring cups and spoons

Silicone spatula

Splatter screen

Ladle

Wide-mouth funnel

Towel or drying rack

recipe continues

01 **Place a plate in your freezer.** This chilled plate comes in handy at Step 17 when ensuring your marmalade has set and is ready to be ladled into your jars.

02 **Prepare your water-boiling canning pot.** Refer to Setting Up Your Water-Boiling Canning Pot on page 48.

03 **Ready your sterilized jars.** Once your canning pot has boiled for 5 minutes, remove the jars and rings. Remove lids from the saucepan. They're going to be hot to the touch, so use a jar lifter to protect your hands. Allow the jars, rings, and lids to cool.

04 **Rinse your oranges in cool water.**

05 **Quarter your oranges.** Cut each orange vertically into four pieces.

06 **Peel your oranges.** Place the peel, or rind, of each orange in a large bowl as you work your way through them. Place the pulp of each orange in your blender. Be sure to remove any loose or large pieces of inner (white) pith.

07 **Cut your rinds.** Cut strips ½–1 inch in length and ⅛ inch in width. Discard or compost the triangular tips of each piece of rind as you cut it into strips.

08 **Place your rinds in your large pot.** Add 3 cups of water, and bring to a low boil. Boil for 15 minutes. Use your spatula to slowly stir. Complete Step 09 as your rinds boil.

09 **Add your lemon juice to your blender.** While your rinds boil, blend the pulps of your oranges with your lemon juice.

10 *Back to your rinds!* Drain your rinds using your strainer. Do not rinse. Place your rinds back in your large pot.

11 **Pour your blended oranges into your pot containing your rinds.** Begin to heat your oranges on low to medium. Use your spatula to begin slowly stirring. Do not boil.

12 **Add your sugar or granulated monk fruit sweetener.** Continue stirring. Include any marmalade that has made its way up the sides of your pot.

13 **Add your vanilla bean paste.** As you continue stirring, add your vanilla bean paste teaspoon by teaspoon. Still include any marmalade that has made its way up the sides of your pot.

14 **Add your chia seeds.** Continue stirring. Still include any marmalade that has made its way up the sides of your pot.

15 **Boil your marmalade.** Increase heat to bring marmalade to a low, gentle boil. Boil for 5 minutes. Stir continuously. Use your splatter screen if needed.

16 **Remove any foam that has accumulated on the surface of your marmalade.**

17 **Make sure your marmalade has set.** Refer to How to Detect the Setting Point of Jam and Marmalade on page 53.

18 **Transfer your marmalade into jars.** Your marmalade will be very hot, so do this carefully. Use your funnel to guide each pour, and use a ladle or a measuring cup to transfer your marmalade. Fill each jar to the lowest part of the jar's mouth, about ½ inch below the rim.

19 **Remove air bubbles.** If you see any bubbles in the jars, use a spatula to guide them out.

20 **Tidy up.** Wipe your jars clean, especially the rims, with a warm, damp towel.

21 **Add your lids and rings.** Tighten.

22 **Process your marmalade.** Submerge your jars into your water-boiling canning pot. Allow them to boil for 10 minutes. Begin your timer once your water is boiling. Adjust for altitude if needed. Refer to The Science and Safety of Canning on page 36.

23 **Cool.** Carefully remove your jars from the water using your jar lifter, and set them on a towel or drying rack to cool.

24 **Ensure they have sealed.** Once cooled, either listen for your jar to "pop," an audible indication it has sealed, or push the center of the lid to see if it pops up and down. If it *doesn't*, it's sealed! Date your jar, and store for up to a year. If the lid *does* pop up and down, it did *not* seal. Simply put that jar in your refrigerator, and enjoy within a month.

GRAPEFRUIT MARMALADE

Steps: 22
Yield: Approximately 4 8-ounce jars

Grapefruits became more a part of my diet after I met Jared. While I did not eat many grapefruits growing up, I've enjoyed them throughout the past decade alongside Jared, who loves them! Grapefruit Marmalade adds pizzazz and dimension to any meal. The inherent bitterness of grapefruit combined with heat and sugar is an absolute delight.

MAKE IT YOUR OWN

More than other citrus fruits, grapefruit contains a large amount of inner (white) pith. You can remove the pith or leave it intact.

By removing the pith, you will reduce the bitterness of your marmalade. The pith itself significantly contributes to the bitterness of grapefruit. If you remove the pith, I recommend deconstructing your grapefruits differently than what I have written below. Instead of cutting your grapefruits into quarters at Step 05, first peel your whole grapefruits using a vegetable peeler. (The rind you peel away is what you will cut into strips at Step 07.) Then, carefully slice away as much of the pith as possible that remains on the body, or pulp, of your grapefruits using a knife. Finally, quarter the bodies of each grapefruit. Using your fingers, pull away any remaining pith. This direction will *reduce* the bitterness of your marmalade.

By leaving the pith intact, you will reduce waste and capture the inherent bitterness of grapefruit when creating this marmalade. Personally, I leave the pith intact. This direction will *preserve* the bitterness of your marmalade.

INGREDIENTS

2 pounds grapefruits

3 cups water

2 tablespoons lemon juice

2 cups sugar

EQUIPMENT & TOOLS

4 8-ounce jars, rings, and lids

Plate

Water-boiling canning pot

Rack

Jar lifter

Saucepan

Thermometer

Strainer

Cutting board

Knife

Large bowl

Blender

Large pot

Measuring cups and spoons

Silicone spatula

Splatter screen

Ladle

Wide-mouth funnel

Towel or drying rack

recipe continues

01 **Place a plate in your freezer.** This chilled plate comes in handy at Step 15 when ensuring your marmalade has set and is ready to be ladled into your jars.

02 **Prepare your water-boiling canning pot.** Refer to Setting Up Your Water-Boiling Canning Pot on page 48.

03 **Ready your sterilized jars.** Once your canning pot has boiled for 5 minutes, remove the jars and rings. Remove lids from the saucepan. They're going to be hot to the touch, so use a jar lifter to protect your hands. Allow the jars, rings, and lids to cool.

04 **Rinse your grapefruits in cool water.**

05 **Quarter your grapefruits.** Cut each grapefruit in half vertically, and then cut each half in half vertically once more.

06 **Peel your grapefruits.** Place the peel, or rind, of each grapefruit in your large bowl as you work your way through your full batch of grapefruits. Place the pulp of each grapefruit in your blender. Be sure to remove any loose or large pieces of inner (white) pith. Do your best to remove all seeds using your fingers.

07 **Cut your rinds.** Cut strips ½–1-inch in length and ⅛ inch in width. Discard or compost the triangular tips of each piece of rind as you cut it into strips.

08 **Place your rinds in your large pot.** Add 3 cups of water, and bring to a low boil. Boil for 15 minutes. Use your spatula to slowly stir. Complete Step 09 as your rinds boil.

09 **Add your lemon juice to your blender.** While your rinds boil, blend the pulps of your grapefruits with your lemon juice.

10 *Back to your rinds!* Drain your rinds using your strainer. Do not rinse. Place your rinds back in your large pot.

11 **Pour your blended grapefruits into your large pot containing your rinds.** Begin to heat your grapefruits on low to medium. Use your spatula to continue slowly stirring. Do not boil.

12 **Add your sugar.** As you continue stirring, add your sugar cup by cup. Include any marmalade that has made its way up the sides of your pot.

13 **Boil your marmalade.** Increase heat to bring marmalade to a low, gentle boil. Boil for 5 minutes. Stir continuously. Use your splatter screen if needed.

14 **Remove any foam that has accumulated on the surface of your marmalade.**

15 **Make sure your marmalade has set.** Refer to How to Detect the Setting Point of Jam and Marmalade on page 53.

16 **Transfer your marmalade into jars.** Your marmalade will be very hot, so do this carefully. Use your funnel to guide each pour, and use a ladle or a measuring cup to transfer your marmalade. Fill each jar to the lowest part of the jar's mouth, about ½ inch below the rim.

17 **Remove air bubbles.** If you see any bubbles in the jars, use a spatula to guide them out.

18 **Tidy up.** Wipe your jars clean, especially the rims, with a warm, damp towel.

19 **Add your lids and rings.** Tighten.

20 **Process your marmalade.** Submerge your jars into your water-boiling canning pot. Allow them to boil for 10 minutes. Begin your timer once your water is boiling. Adjust for altitude if needed. Refer to The Science and Safety of Canning on page 36.

21 **Cool.** Carefully remove your jars from the water using your jar lifter, and set them on a towel or drying rack to cool.

22 **Ensure they have sealed.** Once cooled, either listen for your jar to "pop," an audible indication it has sealed, or push the center of the lid to see if it pops up and down. If it *doesn't*, it's sealed! Date your jar, and store for up to a year. If the lid *does* pop up and down, it did *not* seal. Simply put that jar in your refrigerator, and enjoy within a month.

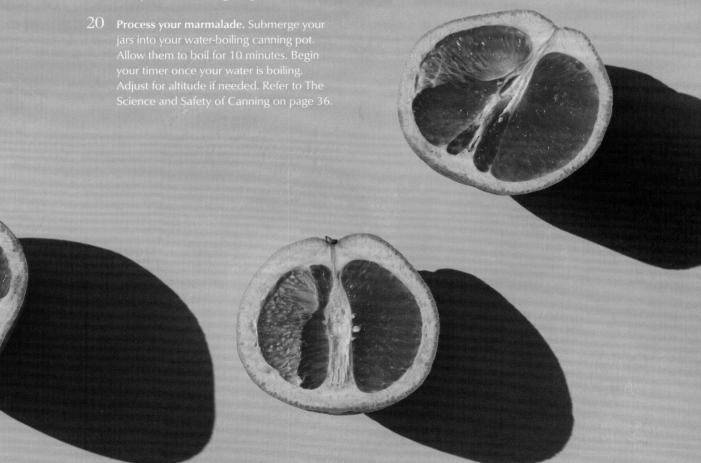

LEMON BASIL MARMALADE

Steps: 25
Yield: Approximately 4 8-ounce jars

When I was pregnant with Sullivan, I craved two things: citrus and comfort. I squeezed fresh lemon juice into a warm cup of water every morning and cool glasses of water throughout every day. I dressed as comfortably as possible and found myself enjoying foods from childhood, such as Luigi's Real Italian Ice. I added touches of lemon and lime to any food or drink that welcomed them.

Lemon Basil Marmalade is *the* marmalade I wish I had when I was growing my son. It is both citrusy and comforting. This marmalade can be paired with the most indulgent of foods, such as cakes, scones, and other baked goods. It can also be served alongside a spread of delicious cheeses. I recommend using Meyer lemons.

MAKE IT YOUR OWN

You can increase the amount of fresh basil by 1 tablespoon for a total of 3 tablespoons. You can also omit the basil for a classic lemon marmalade.

INGREDIENTS

2 pounds lemons

3 cups water

2 tablespoons lemon juice

2 cups sugar

2 tablespoons fresh basil, finely chopped and loosely packed

EQUIPMENT & TOOLS

4 8-ounce jars, rings, and lids

Plate

Water-boiling canning pot

Rack

Jar lifter

Saucepan

Thermometer

Strainer

Cutting board

Knife

Large bowl

Blender

Large pot

Measuring cups and spoons

Silicone spatula

Splatter screen

Ladle

Wide-mouth funnel

Towel or drying rack

recipe continues

01 **Place a plate in your freezer.** This chilled plate comes in handy at Step 18 when ensuring your marmalade has set and is ready to be ladled into your jars.

02 **Prepare the water-boiling canning pot.** Refer to Setting Up Your Water-Boiling Canning Pot on page 48.

03 **Ready your sterilized jars.** Once your canning pot has boiled for 5 minutes, remove the jars and rings. Remove lids from the saucepan. They're going to be hot to the touch, so use a jar lifter to protect your hands. Allow the jars, rings, and lids to cool.

04 **Rinse your lemons in cool water.**

05 **Rinse your basil in cool water.**

06 **Finely chop your basil.** Briefly set aside.

07 **Quarter your lemons.** Cut each lemon vertically into four pieces.

08 **Peel your lemons.** Place the peel, or rind, of each lemon in a large bowl. Place the pulp of each lemon in your blender. Be sure to remove any large pieces of inner (white) pith. Do your best to remove all seeds using your fingers.

09 **Cut your rinds.** Cut strips ½–1 inch in length and ⅛ inch in width. Discard or compost the triangular tips of each piece of rind as you cut it into strips.

10 **Place your rinds in your large pot.** Add 3 cups of water, and bring to a low boil. Boil for 15 minutes. Use your spatula to slowly stir. Complete Step 11 as your rinds boil.

11 **Add your lemon juice to your blender.** While your rinds boil, blend the pulps of your lemons with your lemon juice.

12 *Back to your rinds!* Drain your rinds using a strainer. Do not rinse. Place your rinds back in your large pot.

13 **Pour your blended lemons into your large pot containing your rinds.** Begin to heat your lemons on low to medium. Use your spatula to continue slowly stirring. Do not boil.

14 **Add your basil.** As you continue stirring, add your basil tablespoon by tablespoon. Include any marmalade that has made its way up the sides of your pot.

15 **Add your sugar.** As you continue stirring, add your sugar cup by cup. Still include any marmalade that has made its way up the sides of your pot.

16 **Boil your marmalade.** Increase heat to bring marmalade to a low, gentle boil. Boil for 10 minutes. Stir continuously. Use your splatter screen if needed.

17 **Remove any foam that has accumulated on the surface of your marmalade.**

18 **Make sure your marmalade has set.** Refer to How to Detect the Setting Point of Jam and Marmalade on page 53.

19 **Transfer your marmalade into jars.** Your marmalade will be very hot, so do this carefully. Use your funnel to guide each pour, and use a ladle or a measuring cup to transfer your marmalade. Fill each jar to the lowest part of the jar's mouth, about ½ inch below the rim.

20 **Remove air bubbles.** If you see any bubbles in the jars, use a spatula to guide them out.

21 **Tidy up.** Wipe your jars clean, especially the rims, with a warm, damp towel.

22 **Add your lids and rings.** Tighten.

23 **Process your marmalade.** Submerge your jars into your water-boiling canning pot. Allow them to boil for 10 minutes. Begin your timer once your water is boiling. Adjust for altitude if needed. Refer to The Science and Safety of Canning on page 36.

24 **Cool.** Carefully remove your jars from the water using your jar lifter, and set them on a towel or drying rack to cool.

25 **Ensure they have sealed.** Once cooled, either listen for your jar to "pop," an audible indication it has sealed, or push the center of the lid to see if it pops up and down. If it *doesn't*, it's sealed! Date your jar, and store for up to a year. If the lid *does* pop up and down, it did *not* seal. Simply put that jar in your refrigerator, and enjoy within a month.

SATSUMA RUM MARMALADE

Steps: 24
Yield: Approximately 4 8-ounce jars

Citrus season! We welcome it with open palms in our household. Oranges! Tangerines! Kumquats! *Satsumas!* They allow the longest days of winter to feel warmer, delicious, and more alive.

MAKE IT YOUR OWN

Feelin' boozy? You can increase the amount of rum to your preferred taste. Add 1 additional tablespoon of rum at a time, and taste after each addition. Next, I typically use Gran Marnier as my orange liqueur, but you can use your personal favorite. You can also increase the amount of orange liqueur if you prefer a stronger orange flavor (*and smell!*). Add ½ additional tablespoon of orange liqueur at a time, and taste after each addition.

INGREDIENTS

2 pounds satsumas

3 cups water

2 tablespoons lemon juice

3 cups sugar

2 tablespoons rum

½ tablespoon orange liquor

EQUIPMENT & TOOLS

4 8-ounce jars, rings, and lids

Plate

Water-boiling canning pot

Rack

Jar lifter

Saucepan

Thermometer

Strainer

Cutting board

Knife

Large bowl

Blender

Large pot

Measuring cups and spoons

Silicone spatula

Splatter screen

Ladle

Wide-mouth funnel

Towel or drying rack

recipe continues

01 **Place a plate in your freezer.** This chilled plate comes in handy at Step 17 when ensuring your marmalade has set and is ready to be ladled into your jars.

02 **Prepare your water-boiling canning pot.** Refer to Setting Up Your Water-Boiling Canning Pot on page 48.

03 **Ready your sterilized jars.** Once your canning pot has boiled for 5 minutes, remove the jars and rings. Remove lids from the saucepan. They're going to be hot to the touch, so use a jar lifter to protect your hands. Allow the jars, rings, and lids to cool.

04 **Rinse your satsumas in cool water.**

05 **Peel your satsumas.** Place the peel, or rind, of each satsuma in your large bowl as you work your way through your full batch of satsumas. Place the pulp of each satsuma in your blender. Be sure to remove any large pieces of inner (white) pith.

06 **Cut your rinds.** Cut strips ½–1 inch in length and ⅛ inch in width. Discard or compost the triangular tips of each piece of rind as you cut it into strips.

07 **Place your rinds in your large pot.** Add 3 cups of water, and bring to a low boil. Boil for 10 minutes. Use your spatula to slowly stir. Complete Step 08 as your rinds boil.

08 **Add your lemon juice to your blender.** While your rinds boil, blend the pulps of your satsumas with your lemon juice.

09 *Back to your rinds!* Drain your rinds using your strainer. Do not rinse. Place your rinds back in your large pot.

10 **Pour your blended satsumas into your large pot containing your rinds.** Begin to heat your satsumas on low to medium. Use your spatula to continue slowly stirring. Do not boil.

11 **Add your sugar.** As you continue stirring, add your sugar cup by cup. Include any marmalade that has made its way up the sides of your pot.

12 **Boil your marmalade.** Increase heat to bring marmalade to a low, gentle boil. Boil for 10 minutes. Stir continuously. Use your splatter screen if needed.

13 **Once your marmalade has boiled for 10 minutes, reduce heat.** Add your rum tablespoon by tablespoon. Slowly stir, and fully incorporate.

14 **Add your Gran Marnier.** Slowly stir, and fully incorporate.

15 **Boil your marmalade once more.** Increase your heat to bring your marmalade to a low, gentle boil for an additional 10 minutes.

16 **Remove foam that has accumulated on the surface of your marmalade.**

17 **Make sure your marmalade has set.** Refer to How to Detect the Setting Point of Jam and Marmalade on page 53.

18 **Transfer your marmalade into jars.** Your marmalade will be very hot, so do this carefully. Use your funnel to guide each pour, and use a ladle or a measuring cup to transfer your marmalade. Fill each jar to the lowest part of the jar's mouth, about ½ inch below the rim.

19 **Remove air bubbles.** If you see any bubbles in the jars, use a spatula to guide them out.

20 **Tidy up.** Wipe your jars clean, especially the rims, with a warm, damp towel.

21 **Add your lids and rings.** Tighten.

22 **Process your marmalade.** Submerge your jars into your water-boiling canning pot. Allow them to boil for 10 minutes. Begin your timer once your water is boiling. Adjust for altitude if needed. Refer to The Science and Safety of Canning on page 36.

23 **Cool.** Carefully remove your jars from the water using your jar lifter, and set them on a towel or drying rack to cool.

24 **Ensure they have sealed.** Once cooled, either listen for your jar to "pop," an audible indication it has sealed, or push the center of the lid to see if it pops up and down. If it *doesn't*, it's sealed! Date your jar, and store for up to a year. If the lid *does* pop up and down, it did *not* seal. Simply put that jar in your refrigerator, and enjoy within a month.

FREEZING RECIPES

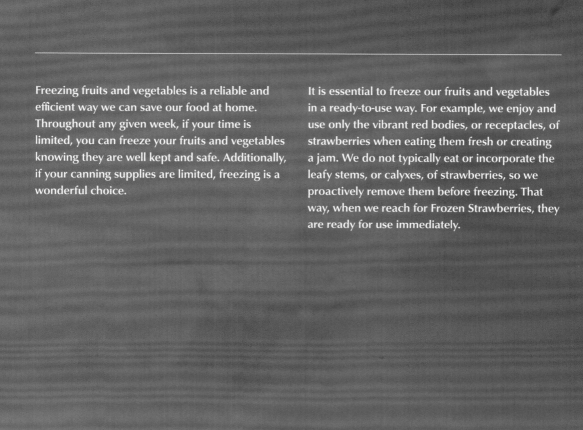

Freezing fruits and vegetables is a reliable and efficient way we can save our food at home. Throughout any given week, if your time is limited, you can freeze your fruits and vegetables knowing they are well kept and safe. Additionally, if your canning supplies are limited, freezing is a wonderful choice.

It is essential to freeze our fruits and vegetables in a ready-to-use way. For example, we enjoy and use only the vibrant red bodies, or receptacles, of strawberries when eating them fresh or creating a jam. We do not typically eat or incorporate the leafy stems, or calyxes, of strawberries, so we proactively remove them before freezing. That way, when we reach for Frozen Strawberries, they are ready for use immediately.

NOTES FOR FREEZING

Preparation

Although freezing fruits and vegetables requires less time and supplies compared to canning, pickling, and preserving, it is equally important to make sure your kitchen is a space in which you're ready to spend some time before freezing. Refer to How to Use *The Wiley Canning Company Cookbook* on page 24. In addition, it is important to open your freezer and ensure it is organized in a way that will welcome new frozen fruits and vegetables. Finally, one way I love to set my future self up to feel joy is to store my favorite fruit or vegetable in a visible position. That way, I am reminded of what's to come every time I open my freezer. If you were to open my freezer right now, you would see Frozen Strawberries and Frozen Blueberries from Kelley's Berry Farm, my favorite local berry farm, and homegrown kale from dear friends of ours. These are small reminders of great fortunes: access to beautiful, ethical farms and friends who prioritize growing their own food and sharing it with those closest to them.

Storage

Once you have completed your recipe, be sure to date your freezer bags or storage containers. If you use freezer bags, I encourage you to store your frozen produce flat. This creates space efficiency in your freezer and avoids major clumping in each bag. Ensure your storage containers are durable, water resistant, and able to fully seal.

Joy

When family members or close friends visit your home in the future, send them home with a bag or storage container of frozen goodies. It is an easy, inexpensive way to share your seasonal abundance, as well as delicious flavors.

FROZEN BELL PEPPERS

Steps: 7
Yield: 1 baking sheet

Frozen Bell Peppers can enhance a wide variety of meals. You can create an entire dish with bell peppers as a focal point, such as a delicious stir fry, or you can add them to a salad, sandwich, or pizza. You can also turn them into pepper jam, hummus, sauce, or salsa. Bell peppers are an excellent *and useful* choice to freeze every year.

MAKE IT YOUR OWN

You can leave your bell peppers at their original length before freezing, or you can cut them into your preferred size. If you know ahead of time how you would like to use your peppers in the future, I recommend freezing them in a ready-to-use way. You can freeze only one ripeness stage of bell pepper, such as a green pepper, or you can freeze a variety of stages together. I recommend freezing *up to* 4 pounds of bell peppers per baking sheet.

INGREDIENTS

4 pounds bell peppers

EQUIPMENT & TOOLS

Strainer

Cutting board

Knife

Baking sheet

Towel

Gallon-size freezer bags or any freezer-safe storage container

recipe continues

01   **Rinse your peppers in cool water.**

02   **Cut your peppers.** Begin by cutting in a circular motion around the stem, or calyx, of each pepper. Completely remove the stem. Cut each pepper in half vertically, and remove its inner pith and seeds.

03   **Slice each half into pieces that are ¼–½-inch wide.**

04   **Place your peppers on your baking sheet as you slice them.** Cover the entire baking sheet with 1–2 layers of peppers. Gently pat dry with a clean towel.

05   **Freeze.** Set your baking sheet of peppers in your freezer. Allow them to freeze for 24 hours. We use a baking sheet to freeze our peppers because we want to ensure each individual pepper is fully frozen.

06   **Fill your freezer bag(s).** After 24 hours, transfer your frozen peppers from your baking sheet to your bag(s) or storage container(s).

07   **Date and store.** Write the date on each bag or container of peppers, and store flat in your freezer for up to a year.

FROZEN BLUEBERRIES

Steps: 5
Yield: 1 baking sheet

Good news! This recipe can be applied to blueberries (below!), blackberries, raspberries, and grapes. Freezing freshly-picked blueberries is the most assured way to experience local, flavorful berries year-round. This process is relatively quick and results in a bounty of fresh blueberries you can use throughout the year to make smoothies, jams, pies, ice cream toppers, *and more*.

INGREDIENTS
4 pints blueberries

EQUIPMENT & TOOLS
Large bowl

Strainer

Baking sheet

Towel

Gallon-size freezer bags or any freezer-safe storage container

recipe continues

01 **Bathe and rinse your blueberries.** Refer to Bathing Your Berries on page 52.

02 **Place your blueberries on your baking sheet.** Cover the entire baking sheet with 1–2 layers of blueberries. Use multiple baking sheets if needed to avoid exceeding 1–2 layers of blueberries. Gently pat dry with a clean towel.

03 **Freeze.** Set your baking sheet of blueberries in your freezer. Allow them to freeze for 24 hours. We use a baking sheet to freeze our berries because we want to ensure each individual berry is fully frozen. We also want to avoid clumping.

04 **Fill your freezer bag(s).** After 24 hours, transfer frozen blueberries from your baking sheet to your bag(s) or storage container(s).

05 **Date and store.** Write the date on each bag or container of blueberries, and store flat in your freezer for up to a year.

FROZEN GREEN BEANS

Steps: 7
Yield: 1 baking sheet

Green beans were a staple in our home growing up. We often ate green beans with dinner, and every holiday gathering included green bean casserole. More than any other fruit or vegetable, Grandma Trudy froze green beans. You can ultimately serve them as a side, chop them into small pieces to serve atop salads, or incorporate them into a delicious casserole or vegetable medley. They are accessible at farmers' markets and grocery stores and freeze incredibly well.

MAKE IT YOUR OWN

You can leave your green beans at their original length before freezing, or you can cut them into your preferred size. If you know ahead of time how you would like to use your beans in the future, I recommend freezing them in a ready-to-use way. For example, if you prefer to eat them as a side, you can leave them at their original length. If you prefer to create a casserole, you can proactively cut them into smaller pieces. I recommend freezing *up to* 3 pounds of green beans per baking sheet. You can apply this recipe to snap beans and wax beans as well.

INGREDIENTS

3 pounds green beans

EQUIPMENT & TOOLS

Strainer

Cutting board

Knife

Large pot

Large bowl

Slotted spoon

Baking sheet

Towel

Gallon-size freezer bags or any freezer-safe storage container

recipe continues

01 **Rinse your beans in cool water.**

02 **Trim the ends of your beans.**

03 **Blanch your beans.** Fill a large pot with water, and bring to a boil. As you're waiting for the water to begin boiling, fill a large bowl with ice water. (You can also plug your sink and fill it with ice water. Both the boiling water and ice water need to be ready at the same time.) Once the water is boiling, drop your beans into the water for 2 minutes. Start timing after the last bean has been dropped. (Do *not* overcrowd your pot. Move through a couple rounds of blanching if needed.) After 2 minutes, use your slotted spoon to remove your beans from the boiling water, and immediately submerge them in your ice water. Allow them to completely cool.

04 **Transfer your beans to your baking sheet.** Cover the entire baking sheet with 1–2 layers of beans. Gently pat dry with a clean towel.

05 **Freeze.** Set your baking sheet of beans in your freezer. Allow them to freeze for 24 hours. We use a baking sheet to freeze our beans because we want to ensure each individual bean is fully frozen.

06 **Fill your freezer bag(s).** After 24 hours, transfer your frozen beans from your baking sheet to your bag(s) or storage container(s).

07 **Date and store.** Write the date on each bag or container of beans, and store flat in your freezer for up to a year.

FROZEN STRAWBERRIES

Steps: 6
Yield: 1 baking sheet

There is no limit to my love for freshly-picked strawberries. Our kitchen feels complete and more joyful when there are ready-to-eat strawberries in our refrigerator, Frozen Strawberries in our freezer, and 8-ounce jars of Strawberry Jam in our pantry. Freezing freshly-picked strawberries is a simple way to enjoy their irreplaceable flavor year-round. Frozen Strawberries can be used to make smoothies right away, or they can be thawed to make jam, pies, *and more*. You can also incorporate them into yogurt or oatmeal for a lively breakfast.

**MAKE
IT YOUR
OWN**

You can leave your strawberries whole before freezing, or you can cut them into halves or quarters. If you know ahead of time how you would like to use your strawberries in the future, I recommend freezing them in a ready-to-use way. For example, if you prefer to use them in a refreshing smoothie each morning, I recommend cutting them into quarters before freezing. You can freeze your strawberries on their own, or you can add additional berries to create a berry medley. One great way to freeze strawberries is among smoothie-ready ingredients. Add frozen blackberries, blueberries, mango, or banana to your freezer bags or freezer-safe storage containers to set yourself up for a smoothie-ready morning.

INGREDIENTS
2 quarts strawberries

EQUIPMENT & TOOLS
Large bowl

Strainer

Knife

Cutting board

Baking sheet

Towel

Gallon-size freezer bags or any freezer-safe storage container

recipe continues

01 **Bathe and rinse your strawberries.** Refer to Bathing Your Berries on page 52.

02 **Hull your strawberries.** In other words, remove the leafy cap, or calyx, from each strawberry.

03 **Place your strawberries on your baking sheet.** Cover the entire baking sheet with a single layer of strawberries. Use multiple baking sheets if needed to avoid stacking or piling strawberries. Gently pat dry with a clean towel.

04 **Freeze.** Set your baking sheet of strawberries in your freezer. Allow them to freeze for 24 hours. We use a baking sheet to freeze our berries because we want to ensure each individual berry is fully frozen. We also want to avoid clumping.

05 **Fill your freezer bag(s).** After 24 hours, transfer your frozen strawberries from your baking sheet to your bag(s) or storage container(s).

06 **Date and store.** Write the date on each bag or container of strawberries, and store flat in your freezer for up to a year.

INGREDIENTS

1 dozen ears of corn

EQUIPMENT & TOOLS

Strainer

Large pot

2 large bowls

Tongs

Cutting board

Knife

2 quart-size freezer bags or any freezer-safe storage container

recipe continues

FROZEN SWEET CORN

Steps: 7
Yield: Approximately 2 quart-size freezer bags

As I sat down to write this recipe, my cousin, Tiffany, sent two photos of my late grandfather, Grandpa Don, to our family text thread. I replied and said, "I can smell Grandpa as I look at these photos."

Why is it that when I see his photo, I can smell the Ohio dirt on his hands and forearms mixed with sweat and a trace of Dial's gold soap? Why can I so clearly see his jaw move side to side as butterscotch candy clacks between his teeth?

Why can I also taste sweet corn? My eardrums and hands tingle as I think about shucking sweet corn on his concrete porch beneath the golden sun. This task is simple, but it had to be taught to me. Of course, Grandpa Don taught me the best way to shuck sweet corn.

"You peel the husk from the top. Get it nice and good. See all 'ese little hairs here? Get 'em. You can leave the handle so it's easier to eat. That's called 'the shank'. We'll call it 'the handle', though. Now listen. Get it nice and good. Get it nice and clean."

MAKE IT YOUR OWN

Sweet corn is at its absolute prime flavor as soon as it is picked. Its milky sugars begin converting into less flavorful starches as soon as it is pulled from the earth. When sweet corn is in season in your area, go to your local farmers' market, and ask a sweet corn vendor when their corn is typically picked. Tell the vendor you'd like to buy as close to when it is picked as possible. You'd like do this because you want to cook it or freeze it as close to when it is picked as possible. You want to capture as much of its inherent sweetness as possible, and you can.

01 **Shuck your corn.** Find a comfortable place to sit and shuck outside, and completely remove the husk from your corn.

02 **Rinse your corn.** Rinse to remove excess silk. Briefly set aside.

03 **Blanch your corn.** Fill a large pot with water, and bring to a boil. (Use a pot large enough to fit full ears of corn.) As you're waiting for the water to begin boiling, fill a large bowl with ice water. (You can also plug your sink and fill it with ice water. Both the boiling water and ice water need to be ready at the same time.) Once the water is boiling, drop your corn into the water for 4 minutes. Start timing after the last ear has been dropped. After 4 minutes, use your tongs to remove your corn from the boiling water, and immediately submerge it in your ice water. Allow each ear to completely cool.

Hold each ear tightly, and notice if you feel any heat. You want to feel no heat at all.

04 **Cut your corn off the cob.** Once the ear has completely cooled, carefully cut the corn off the cob, and begin to fill your second large bowl.

05 **Savor the sweetness.** Run the back of your knife's blade along the bare corn cob to extract any excess sweet and creamy liquid from the cob itself.

06 **Fill your freezer bag(s).** Once you've cut the corn off the cobs, fill each bag ½ full. Lay flat, and push as much air as possible out of the bag before sealing.

07 **Date and store.** Write the date on each bag of corn, and store flat in your freezer for up to a year.

CLOSING STATEMENT

I write my best work when I'm confined to a single seat in a Boeing 737. This setting, unfailingly, helps me access the mind with which I write. It is not the mind with which I parent, and it is not the mind with which I cook or teach or run. It is the mind behind a locked door on the top floor of a secluded house, and I attempt to access it each day to write as if my life depends on it.

When I open that door, I might find a cold, bare room. Or, I might find a warm, inviting room, one filled with complete sentences that acutely describe my specific emotion or experience. No matter what I find, I write. Traveling in an airplane, thirty thousand feet above Earth, helps me unlock this door more quickly than any other setting. I know this to be true. I sit still. There is little distraction. Cellular service is unavailable.

I faced this truth when I found myself three weeks away from my final deadline for *The Wiley Canning Company Cookbook* with a mountain of pages yet to create. As a new mother, I had not yet learned how to best prioritize my day. I had not yet learned how to live and create well despite my exhaustion. I had not yet learned how to quiet my mind as it buzzed with excitement, worry, and curiosity about my infant son. Day by day, I let my work slip through my fingers, and time was running out. With only three weeks left, I knew I had to make a serious change. I needed to sit still, reduce distraction, and restrict my phone use. I had to access the mind behind a locked door on the top floor of a secluded house, the mind with which I write. To do so, I had to overcome the fear and vulnerability I felt to be apart from my son.

"I can do this," I repeatedly said. "And I must."

I boarded a Boeing 737 to Albuquerque, New Mexico and traveled to a small village named Galisteo. For five days, I found myself alone in the golden desert in a one-bedroom casita. There was a small desk, a single chair, and limited cellular service.

There, I wrote. I wrote. And I wrote.

For this brief moment in time, I successfully compartmentalized my fear and vulnerability, and I poured my mind and heart into my work. *The Wiley Canning Company Cookbook* mattered entirely to me. I created that mountain of pages. I felt relieved. I felt proud.

Now, it was time to travel home to my son. I needed to see him, hold him, and allow my mind to, once again, buzz about him. As I sat at my gate in Albuquerque to travel home, I continued to write. It was, after all, my goal to make the most of my time away.

My work was suddenly interrupted when the gate attendant began an announcement with trepidation in her voice. She said, "I have a very unfortunate announcement. Please remember I am only the person communicating this decision to you. I have no control over the decision itself."

"What in the world could this be?" I wondered.

"All remaining flights out of Albuquerque have been canceled. There are currently no available flights for three days. In addition, all hotels in Albuquerque are sold out due to our annual International Balloon Festival. We will do our absolute best to ensure you have a place to sleep and eat until we are able to find a flight for you."

Gulp.

I sat in sheer disbelief as I watched hundreds of panicked travelers form a rapidly growing line. I could not remain apart from my son for three additional days. Not only would it have been difficult emotionally, but it also would have been difficult logistically due to childcare needs. The day before, I wrote as if my life depended on it. Now, I had to problem solve as if my life depended on it.

Luckily, there was a rental car available. I needed to quickly reserve it, map my route, and ensure I had a full charge on my phone. I had to access the mind with which *I endure*, the same mind with which I run. To do so, I had to overcome the fear and vulnerability I felt to complete a cross-country drive through the black of night.

"I can do this," I repeatedly said. "And I must."

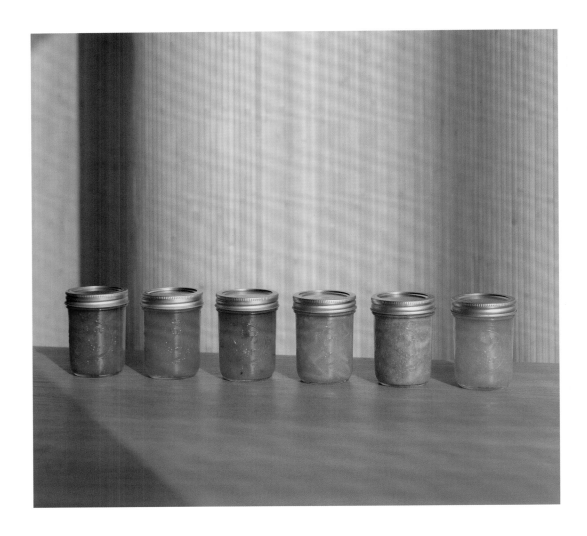

I rented a Nissan Kick and traveled toward Nashville, Tennessee as the western sun met the horizon behind me. For eighteen hours, I found myself alone on the highways of New Mexico, Texas, Oklahoma, Arkansas, and Tennessee. There were wind farms, plains, and dark, infinite skies.

There, I focused. I focused. And I focused.

For this brief moment in time, I successfully compartmentalized my fear and vulnerability, and I poured my mind and energy into the drive. Traveling home to my son mattered entirely to me. I completed that cross-country drive through the black of night. I felt relieved. I was home.

In a span of five days alone, my work mattered entirely to me, and my son mattered entirely to me. In one moment, I chose to board a Boeing 737 to Albuquerque, New Mexico and write as if my life depended on it, and in the next moment, I chose to rent a Nissan Kick and drive as if my life depended on it. As human beings, we pursue one instinctual experience after another. We make one careful decision after another. We grapple with one thought-provoking paradox after another. We do so much more than choose to board a Boeing 737, despite the fear and vulnerability we feel to be apart from our children. We do so much more than rent a Nissan Kick, despite the fear and vulnerability we feel to complete a cross-country drive through the black of night.

We pursue our first 5k because we believe it will bring us a tremendous sense of pride, despite feeling nervous, even unqualified, to step into running shoes. We decide to call our dying grandmother to tell her how much we love her because this might be our final chance, despite the excruciating heartbreak of that call. We find heroic strength in the profound love we have for our children, despite being brought to our knees by exhaustion and overwhelm. We begin to write our first book, despite an endless list of unknowns and quiet insecurities.

We break, and we rebuild. We second-guess, and we fully commit. We give away our love, and it finds its way back to us. We pursue and accept the complexity of our lives, and we do the best we can.

This is not easy. This is not comfortable. This is not predictable or tidy. The complexity of our lives tests our humanity at times, and it celebrates our humanity at others. It allows us to create a mountain of pages, and it allows us to complete a cross-country drive. It is what makes us authors, and it is what makes us mothers.

My wish for each of us is to know, without a shadow of doubt, that our work matters entirely when it matters most. My wish for each of us is to know, without a shadow of doubt, that our people—our children, partners, parents, grandparents, friends, and colleagues—matter entirely when they matter most. We must board the Boeing 737 when our work matters most, and we must rent the Nissan Kick when our people matter most. We must pursue our first 5k. We must call our grandmother. We must fall to our knees, and we must begin our first book.

We must pursue and accept the complexity of our lives, and we must do the best we can. In doing so, we honor every single ingredient that makes our miraculous lives so beautifully ordinary and so very delicious.

KEY TERMS

Acetic acid:
Ethanoic acid, CH_3COOH. Acetic acid is used to make distilled white and apple cider vinegars. Vinegar is typically 5% acetic acid.

Acidic:
Having a pH below 7.0 on a scale of 0.0–14.0. Sour or bitter in taste. The closer to 0.0, the more acidic the food. The closer to 7.0, the lower the acidity. Any food above 7.0 is considered alkaline, or basic. Any food between 4.6 and 7.0 is considered to have low acidity. Lemon juice (pH 2.0–2.6) is often added to recipes to add acidity for safety.

Acidifier:
A food or substance with a pH below 4.6, such as lemon juice or ascorbic acid, added to a recipe to increase its acidity, or decrease its pH.

Agrarian:
Agricultural. Characteristic of or relating to farmers or their way of life. Designed to promote farming or agricultural interests. Relating to the cultivation of lands or fields.

Altitude:
One's height or vertical distance above sea level. Altitude affects air pressure and boiling point. At higher altitudes, air pressure and boiling points are lower. Therefore, at higher altitudes, foods take longer to cook.

Alum:
Potassium aluminum sulfate, $KAl(SO_4)_2 \cdot 12H_2O$. Alum is most commonly used for pickling as its astringent properties thicken and bind the skin or rind of a fruit or vegetable. One popular use is as an additive to increase the crunchiness of pickles.

Apple cider vinegar:
Fermented apple juice. (See fermentation.) Apple cider vinegar is commonly used for pickling and must be at least 5% acidic.

Ascorbic acid:
Vitamin C. Ascorbic acid prevents oxidation, or browning, of fruits and vegetables.

Blanching:
A two-step process that first scalds a fruit or vegetable in boiling water for a brief period of time, then shocks that fruit or vegetable in ice water. Blanching is used to ease the process of peeling the skin off fruits and vegetables.

Boiling point:
The temperature at which a liquid becomes a gas. Boiling point is dependent on material and altitude (air pressure). Most commonly, the boiling point of water at sea level is 212°F, or 100°C.

Brine:
A highly-concentrated solution of water and salt (and oftentimes vinegar and added spices) used to pickle, preserve, or season food.

Canning:
A method of saving food through processed, sealed, and airtight containers.

Canning salt:
Sodium chloride (NaCl). Canning salt, or pickling salt, strictly contains sodium and chloride, does not contain iodine, and is typically finely ground to increase its rate of solubility.

Distilled white vinegar:
Acetic acid and water. (See acetic acid.) Distilled white vinegar is commonly used for pickling and must be at least 5% acidic.

Drip test:
A test commonly used to gauge the setting point of a preserve. A spoon or spatula is dipped into a pot of cooked preserve and held above the pot to observe how quickly or slowly the preserve drips.

Fermentation:
A process through which a microorganism (e.g., yeast or bacteria) converts carbohydrates (e.g., sugar or starch) into an alcohol. In other words, fermentation is the conversion of sugar into alcohol.

Foundation:
A basis, or principle, or an understanding upon which further thought or action is built.

Freezer test:
A test commonly used to gauge the setting point of a jam or marmalade. A spoonful of cooked jam or marmalade is placed on a chilled plate for two minutes. When the preserve is nudged, it should wrinkle if it has set.

Jam:
A gelatinous and spreadable substance made from combining fruits, sugar, water, and heat.

Marmalade:
A gelatinous and spreadable substance made from combining a fruit, its rind, sugar, water, and heat. It is most commonly made from citrus fruits.

Pectin:
A naturally-occurring polysaccharide found in most fruits and vegetables. Typically, the tougher or sturdier a fruit is, the more pectin it contains. For example, an apple contains more pectin than a raspberry.

Pickling:
A method of saving food through immersion in a brine or vinegar. (See brine, apple cider vinegar, and distilled white vinegar.)

Preserving:
An overarching term meaning to prevent the spoilage of food for a long period of time through canning, pickling, and preserving. Freezing and freeze-drying are two additional methods of preservation. Preserving is also a method of creating jams and marmalades by using fruits or vegetables, sugar, and heat.

Setting point:
The point at which a preserve has reached desired consistency, or viscosity. A preserve's setting point can be tested via the drip test or freezer test. (See drip test and freezer test.)

Steward:
One who thoughtfully, respectfully, and honorably cares for or manages something valuable.

Sugar:
A sweet and soluble carbohydrate naturally found in fruits and vegetables. An additive.

Viscosity:
A measure of consistency, typically thickness, commonly used when making preserves.

RESOURCES

Cookbooks
- *Ball Complete Book of Home Preserving* by Judi Kingry and Lauren Devine
- *Canning in the Modern Kitchen* by Jamie DeMent
- *Canning for a New Generation* by Liana Krissoff
- *Food in Jars* by Marisa McClellan
- *Ball Blue Book Guide to Preserving* by Judy Harrold
- *Heritage* by Sean Brock | Pages 205–235
- *Preserving by the Pint* by Marisa McClellan
- *Tart and Sweet* by Kelly Geary and Jessie Knadler
- *The Amish Canning Cookbook* by Georgia Varozza
- *The Noma Guide to Fermentation* by René Redzepi and David Zilber | Pages 157–209
- *The Peach Truck Cookbook* by Jessica N. Rose and Stephen K. Rose | Pages 245–273

Biographies
- *The Earth Knows My Name* by Patricia Klindienst

Additional
- *The Illustrated Encyclopedia of Fruits, Vegetables, and Herbs* by Barbara Santich and Geoff Bryant
- *An Illustrated Catalogue of American Fruits and Nuts* by The U.S. Department of Agriculture Pomological Watercolor Collection

Online Resources
- The website for Native Land Digital; Native-land.ca
- The website for First Nations Development Institute; Firstnations.org
- The website for the National Museum of the American Indian, Smithsonian Institution; Americanindian.si.edu
- The website for the National Congress of American Indians; Ncai.org
- The website for the Bureau of Indian Affairs; Bia.gov
- *Indigenizing the News*; Indigenizingthenews.com

CITATIONS

Ball Corporation. n.d. "The History of Ball." Ball. Accessed August 05, 2022. https://www.ball.com/our-company/our-story/history-timeline

Eckert, Allan W. 1993. *A Sorrow in Our Heart: The Life of Tecumseh.* New York: Bantam Books.

Greenspan, Jesse. 2018. "6 Things You May Not Know About Tecumseh." History. https://www.history.com/news/6-things-you-may-not-know-about-tecumseh

Klindienst, Patricia. 2006. *The Earth Knows My Name: Food, Culture, and Sustainability in Ethnic American Gardens.* Boston: Beacon Press.

Lord, Barry. 2014. *Art & Energy: How Culture Changes.* Washington, DC: The AAM Press.

McClellan, Marisa. 2018. "Canning 101: How to Swap Citric Acid for Lemon Juice and Vice Versa." Food in Jars. October 25, 2018. https://foodinjars.com/blog/canning-101-how-to-swap-citric-acid-for-lemon-juice-and-vice-versa/

National Center for Home Food Preservation. 2017. "Sterilization of Empty Jars." Home Canning: Jars and Lids, National Center for Home Food Preservation. Reviewed February 2, 2017. https://nchfp.uga.edu/how/can_01/sterile_jars.html

Ohio History Connection. n.d. Ohio History Central. Accessed August 05, 2022. https://ohiohistorycentral.org

PBS Western Reserve. "One State, Many Nations: Native Americas of Ohio." Multimedia project, 2004, produces by PBS 45 & 49. https://www.pbswesternreserve.org/education/one-state-many-nations-native-americans-of-ohio/

Pruitt, Sarah. 2019. "The Juicy 4,000-Year History of Pickles." History. https://www.history.com/news/pickles-history-timeline

Sullivan, Taira. n.d.a. "How Did We Can? The Evolution of Home Canning Practices." A National Agricultural Digital Exhibit, About, National Agricultural Library. Accessed August 05, 2022. https://www.nal.usda.gov/exhibits/ipd/canning/

USDA (United States Department of Agriculture). 2000. "A Condensed History of American Agriculture 1776–1999." USDA. https://www.usda.gov/sites/default/files/documents/history-american-agriculture.pdf

——. n.d.b. "How Did We Can? The Evolution of Home Canning Practices." A National Agricultural Digital Exhibit, Canning Timeline Table, National Agricultural Library. Accessed August 05, 2022. https://www.nal.usda.gov/exhibits/ipd/canning/timeline-table

ACKNOWLEDGEMENTS

To the Wiley Canning Company community: With all that I am, I thank you. Wiley Canning Company, including this book, would not exist without you. Thank you for believing in me when you did not yet have a tangible reason. I will *never* forget your support. Elizabeth Gilbert said that encouraging words actually place courage within her; they *en-courage* her. The people around you—around me—have the power to drop pieces of courage into us when we need it most. You have done this for me day after day. I promise you I will take great care of Wiley Canning Company and all that is born from it. I will lead with honesty and hope. I will share every celebration and shoulder every misstep. Wiley *is* because we *are*. Thank you.

To Jared: Every single day begins and ends with you. You have and will always bet on *me*, not the work I create. This is an immeasurable act of love. I know that no matter the caliber or success of my work, you will continue to hold me tightly in care and support. Although Wiley is a huge part of our lives, I know it is me, your teammate in all things, and *us* you treasure most. Thank you for being the person to whom I can return again and again knowing I will never be graded or critiqued, only loved and held. My love for you and our family exceeds all else.

To Dad: Your work ethic and energy are limitless. You know the assets and strengths only you can bring to the table, and you own and build upon them. You have taught me to own what makes me *me*. This has given me both power and purpose. Additionally, if I told you I set a goal to cartwheel to the moon wearing a blindfold with a barbell between my feet, you would believe in me. Knowing I can come to you with any idea or goal is precisely what allows me to dream. I can think imaginatively because you foster and affirm my curious mind. I am so very proud to be your

daughter. I am so very proud to own my assets and strengths because you first owned yours.

To Mom: My most vivid memory of my adolescence is the sight of you receiving the doctorate you earned with a full-time job and three children. You exemplify that I, too, can lace up my shoes and chase down my dreams no matter my stage of life. More than any award, accolade, or championship of any celebrity, this accomplishment of yours has influenced me most. Your endurance is exceptional. I am so very proud to be your daughter. I am so very proud to chase down my dreams because you first chased yours.

To Sarah: You and Amy are part of my foundation. You read every word I write. You hold me when I crumble, and you celebrate me when I succeed. Thank you for playing with Sullivan at a moment's notice to allow me to finish a recipe. Thank you for showing up at our door with champagne to celebrate small milestones. Thank you for never doubting.

To Amy: You and Sarah are two of my life's greatest gifts. I cannot imagine an existence without the sisterhood I have with you. You bring humor and levity to my life when I need it most. Thank you for waking up before the sunrise with Sullivan to allow me the rest so I could write. Thank you for treating my jam like it's the best jam in the entire world. Thank you for never doubting.

To Jones: You are my favorite company to keep. You are the *most* steadfast and loyal companion. You brought me perspective, comfort, and pure, uninterrupted love as I brought *The Wiley Canning Company Cookbook* to life. As our family grew and changed, and as my work evolved, you remained calm, consistent, and forgiving. You are the best boy, and you complete our family.

A Martha Castillo: Las palabras no pueden expresar mi aprecio por usted. Gracias por unirse a nuestra familia durante un tiempo de transformación. Gracias por amar y cuidar a Sullivan tan bien y hermosamente. Usted es exactamente lo que necesitábamos para alcanzar nuestras metas como familia. Estamos en deuda con usted para siempre. Mil gracias.

To Mary Arwen: I wish everyone I love could have a Mary Arwen in their life. I tossed my most intimate fears and insecurities to you, and you caught them and transformed them. Back to me, you tossed an unhesitating certainty that I could write this book. There was not a single moment you doubted the possibility of it, and this steadfast confidence carried me. You helped me uncover the power within me as a woman, partner, mother, and artist—and to get the job done. You were unwavering.

To Matthew Teague: You sent me the very first email that launched the creation of this book. It was at a time when I was growing my son and becoming a mother, having no idea where or how my treasured work would fit into a new season of my life. You proceeded to treat me with the utmost kindness, respect, and spaciousness. Not only has your belief in me strengthened my belief in myself, but it has also taught me the importance of voicing my belief in others. You took a huge chance on me, and in doing so, you expanded my life, mind, and heart. This book is everything I needed to be the best woman, partner, mother, and artist I could be when at times I felt completely lost. Thank you for this gift. I am forever grateful.

To Josh Nava: What a gift you are to my life and career! You truly do it all. Working with you on *The Wiley Canning Company Cookbook* was, first and foremost, *so much fun.* It was also efficient and gratifying. Thank you for your diligent work, long hours, and perfectly-placed sense of humor. Your talent and craftsmanship encourage me to pursue high standards in my own work.

To Alexandra Callahan: You unfailingly created a peace for me throughout the creation process of *The Wiley Canning Company Cookbook* as my copy editor. You noticed every grammatical mistake and anecdotal wrong turn, and you gently course corrected. This role could not have been filled by just anyone. It had to be you. I am so very grateful for your integral part in this process. This book is far better and clearer because of your touch. I am equally grateful for your example and friendship. If you agree to an endeavor, *you commit.* Your loyalty is unparalleled.

To Lindsay Hess: A wide smile or sense of warmth can draw us to another human. Each creates an initial attraction, no matter how subtle, during a meet-cute. Just like a wide smile or sense of warmth, the design of a book attracts us to it before we begin to read its pages. Your role as a designer was central to the sharing of this book. Your mind's eye created what catches the initial attention of a human. Thank you for your creative openness, attunement, and commitment to every visual detail.

To Elizabeth Pape: You changed the course of my creativity, self-confidence, and identity when you welcomed me into your Berry Hill studio. You therefore changed the course of my life. To me, you are and have always been the best: the best leader, mentor, and arbiter of evocative art, design, and storytelling. I am forever your biggest fan. I am forever on your team. I am forever in awe of your commitment to your self-expression, evolution, and craft.

To My Girlfriends: You believe in me. This will always carry me. Day after day, you clothe me in support, celebration, and love. You are always a place to which to retreat, and you are always a place from which to soar. The winning lottery of my life is the friendships I have with each of you. You are the women who walk me home.

Thanks To:

Sarah and Don Jenney
Trudy and Don Ruehle
Elizabeth Wiley
Kim Jenney (Reegyn and Tanner)
Mary and Rick Griffith
Arthur and Lee Ann O'Leary
Mark McClain
Ben Driskell
Garin and Brooke O'Leary
Katy and Brian Brennan
Charles O'Leary
Rachel Griffith and Taylor Johnson
Anslee Driskell
Mylah Jenney
Rowan Driskell
Logan O'Leary
Elora Brennan
Dorian Brennan
Lindsay Drake
Taylor Feightner
Molly Lonca
Grace Cho
Kyuwon Lee
Kate Davis
Laura Lea Bryant
Adi and Sean Brock
Emily Green
Taylor Thomas
Lydia Plageman
Lauren Watt
Carissa Shapiro

Maggie Raterman
Destiny DeStefano
Chris Martucci
Tiana Gidley
Kylie Nadeau
Emma Esquibel
Emily Thompson
Rebekka Seale
Elise Joseph
Zachary Gray
Amanda LeSaicherre
Max and Alice Goldberg
Kat and Michael Roos
Mr. Weiskopf
Mr. Watson
Mrs. McKibben
Mr. Stepro
Mrs. Wilson
Coach Yunker
Dr. Zimmerman
Dr. Bouchard
Dr. Hanson
Benjamin de Bivort
Kirstin Scott
Emily Leonard
Caroline Randall Williams
Cheryl Strayed
Elizabeth Gilbert
Kate Baer
David Whyte

INDEX

ABOUT THE AUTHOR

Chelsea J. O'Leary is a Nashville-based artist, entrepreneur, and home food preserver. She is the founder and owner of Wiley Canning Company, a company dedicated to canning, pickling, and preserving local and seasonal fruits and vegetables. Chelsea creates recipes and hosts workshops to teach others to can, pickle, and preserve as well. She explores photography through both a film and digital format, and she is especially drawn to photographing fruits and vegetables.

When she is not canning, pickling, preserving, or creating photographs, she values and seeks meaningful, curiosity-driven dialogue with others. She loves to write and run, in the woods or through the city, and she cherishes time spent with her husband, Jared, and son, Sullivan. You might find them at a local farmers' market, park, or nearby wooded trail.

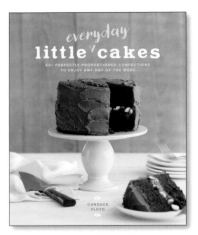

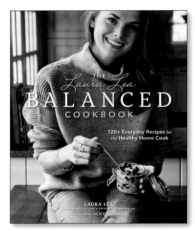